HerStory

What I Learned in My Bathtub…
*and More True Stories on
Life, Love, and Other
Inconveniences*

Indi Zeleny

editor

Adams Media
Avon, Massachusetts

Published by
Adams Media, an F+W Publications Company
57 Littlefield Street, Avon, MA 02322. U.S.A.
www.adamsmedia.com

ISBN: 1-59337-505-0

Printed in the United States of America.

J I H G F E D C B A

Library of Congress Cataloging-in-Publication Data
HerStory / Indi Zeleny, editor.
p.   cm.
ISBN 1-59337-505-0
1. Women—Biography. 2. Women—Psychology.
3. Self-realization in women. I. Title: Her story. II. Zeleny, Indi.
HQ1123.H47 2005
305.4'092—dc22
2005016008

*This book is available at quantity discounts for bulk purchases.
For information, please call 1-800-872-5627.*

For my mother and my daughter

Pim and Parise

whose moments I treasure.

Every single day.

Acknowledgments

No editor is an island, and although at times in my little home office I felt isolated and island-like, I am no exception. I owe a debt of gratitude to so many individuals:

To the hundreds of women writers who bravely shared their lives, loves, and losses with me through the pages of their stories—I wish I could have included all of your wonderful tales in this anthology. And to the final thirty women for sharing their pivotal moments, through these pages, with spirited women everywhere.

To Paula Munier, who trusted and honored me with her brainchild; without her vision, there would be no *HerStory*. And to wise woman Colleen Sell, who advised me every step of the way, but particularly in the high-speed, whiz-bang slide into finish. Many thanks, also, to the great team at Adams Media, especially Kate Epstein.

To my daughter Parise for "working" on her LeapPad and "reading" her books while Mommy plugged away at the computer. And to my son Bridger for nursing and (more rarely) napping while I typed. A huge thank you to my mother Pim Chavasant, my in-laws Nick and Dana Alaga, and my friend Elizabeth Tarozzi for tenderly grandparenting the children while I worked.

And the greatest recognition goes to my husband Randy, who not only bestowed his editorial savvy upon request, but came home from work every afternoon to change diapers, clean house, and feed, entertain, and love the children so I could devote my time to this project; who is that rare man who considers the label "honorary woman" a compliment; who is my true partner in every sense of the word.

Thank you to women and honorary women everywhere.

Contents

Introduction

Truth or Dare. That's what came to mind when I took on the project *HerStory*. *We are asking a lot from these women writers.* But unlike the prepubescent challenge where you would choose between answering an intimate question or performing a daunting feat, *HerStory* demanded both. We wanted women who dared *and* we wanted their true stories.

As a self-conscious girl, I'd always chosen dare. To tell the truth and reveal the hidden me was unthinkable. It would expose my genuine self to the judging eyes of my friends, who, at twelve and thirteen, were unreliable at best. To my pre-teen mind, an honest answer could haunt me to eternity.

So I thought long and hard about *HerStory*. I was the game master. What was I really asking them to do? I was asking them to trust us, to be our friends, our closest friends. To sit down with us on the rug, our backs up against the sofa, bare feet, some wine or a plate of chocolate-chip cookies on the table, and tell us all about it. *What happened? Are you okay? Were you nuts? Oh my God I can't believe you did that! You are amazing. I hope I could do something like that if I were in your shoes.* I was asking them to be brave—a lot braver than I myself had ever been.

So I put the word out to women everywhere, asking for their true tales of the moments that make us. The times when we put our foot down and took a stand. The times when we went for it and opened the doors to the universe. The milestones in women's lives today. And hundreds of stories flooded in.

These stories became my adoptive family. I ate, drank, and slept in the worlds of these everyday women as they made their way through the ordinary to the bizarre to the most grueling circumstances. I felt the strength of their convictions, the weight of their choices, and the joy of their victories—large and small. Whether it was an exhausted new mom getting that bath she so desperately needed or a woman who literally piloted a ship through life-threatening, stormy seas; one pursuing the love of her life or another burying a living ex-husband—these women overcame adversity and unstuck the sticking places in their lives to emerge better, stronger, happier. And, being the fabulous gender that they are, they more often than not achieved this end with grace and humor.

Then, as I read through every single story, I found a common thread. More than grit, gumption, and determination, there was a level of honesty and openness from these women that floored me. They exposed their mishaps and foibles, their "dirty little secrets," their less-than-perfect sex lives and their bad parenting moments. Truth or Dare? Oh, yeah, baby. Live and uncensored.

And the stories left us wanting even more. Just like we hate to finish a great novel, to turn that last page and close the book and end forever our connection with the characters we've grown to love, we wanted to know what happened next. Where these women were now and what had come to pass. So we took our "friendship" to an even greater level. We asked all of our

writers to talk to us—like we were best friends at a sleepover—
to divulge the story behind the story, the unseen and intimate
details, the aftermath. The illuminating, emotional, and often-
times hilarious results of these interviews appear in a question-
and-answer format after each story.

Now, when we sit down with this book and immerse ourselves in these stories, we befriend these remarkable, yet ordinary women. Through these stories you will experience when
her guy ran out and left her jobless with two small children;
when her hillbilly in-laws arrived on the doorstep after the birth
of her first baby; when the lonely married woman met her sexy
new neighbor; when the young New Yorker married a real cowboy and left the city for the vast prairie. They speak from their
hearts and assure us that they made it work, perhaps in ways
different from what they had originally intended, but that they
are safe and sane and that they are the better for their coura-
geous choices.

I hope that you will enjoy getting to know these thirty
women writers with their wildly divergent voices and views, and
rejoice in their common ground of laughter, candor, and the
willingness to dive headfirst into life. Their stories celebrate the
moments that help women everywhere deal with the cathartic
stuff of life, and it's my hope that they will inspire you to take
positive action in your own lives. We are no longer girls playing
at Truth or Dare, but full-blown women playing for real. We are
our own game masters. And their stories are our stories—taken
straight from the lives of truthful and daring women everywhere. Together, we create *HerStory*.

Indi Zeleny

What I Learned in My Bathtub

❧

Paula Munier

There are two kinds of people in the world: shower people and bath people. Shower people love the instant gratification a shower provides—a flip of the faucet and there you are naked, warm, happy, pounded on all pores by steaming, streaming, screaming water. People who take showers are sensible, straightforward, proactive—the doers of the world.

Bath people have a more languorous approach to life. A bathtub takes time to fill, and there are all kinds of ways to fill it. You can fill it with bubbles, milk, even champagne. You can toss in herbs, oils, and rubber duckies. You can splash or soak, play or pout, think deep thoughts or think of nothing at all. People who take baths are creative, romantic, secretive—the dreamers of the world.

I am now a bath person.

Friday
3:00 A.M.

The baby whimpers, and I roll over to my husband's empty side of the bed. I cover my head with a pillow and wait to see if he'll go back to sleep. The baby monitor sits on my grandmother's antique dresser next to our bed, crackling as little Greggie shuffles his legs and swings his arms in his crib. I sigh; I know what's coming. My second-born child is gathering his strength for the shriek that will propel me out of this room and into his. Suddenly, it's a wallowing wail in Dolby sound—from the monitor, from the nursery on the other side of the wall, from the hammering in my head. I glance at the clock. My husband will be home from his two-week business trip to Paris in fifteen hours. I get up.

4:00 A.M.

I am back in bed. After an hour of nursing, rocking, burping, and singing, I have surrendered to the inevitable. I lie on my back, the baby snoring on my chest. This is against the rules; everyone from my mother to my pediatrician says that I could roll over in my sleep and suffocate little Greggie, but I did this all the time with his insomniac big sister Alexis and she survived, so I ignore all expert advice. Speaking of Alexis, here she comes, my two-year-old princess, who walked at nine months but only started sleeping through the night five months ago, the week little Greggie was born. She pulls herself onto our bed with an alarming alacrity for a toddler and snuggles up to me. With my arm tucked around her sweet blonde head, she effectively serves as ballast. I won't be rolling over any time soon. Little Greggie will live to see another sleepless night. But will I?

6:00 A.M.

Alexis, the farmer, is up with the sun. She pulls on the torn and stained Red Sox T-shirt that serves as my sexy lingerie these days with chubby, sticky fingers.

"Mommy!" There is an imperiousness to her tone that Queen Elizabeth II would envy. "Mommy! I want Mickey Mouse pancakes!"

I curse my mother under my breath, the perfect grandmother and perfect maker of perfect Mickey Mouse pancakes.

"Ssh! Let's not wake up little Greggie." There is a pleading to my tone that Queen Elizabeth II would not envy. My nipples are cracked and sore from all the nursing, and I'm not looking forward to his next feeding.

Alexis regards her baby brother, still asleep on my heavy breasts, with a disdain only an elder sibling can muster. "He's just a *baby*."

"That's right, honey. He's just a baby. No Mickey Mouse pancakes for him."

Alexis beams. "That's right, honey. No Mickey Mouse pancakes for you!" She pokes him in his tiny ribs with her fat little index finger. Little Greggie wakes up with his trademark wail.

8:00 A.M.

Thank God for *Sesame Street*. I owe my sanity—and my pregnancy weight loss—to this show alone. Alexis loves it; it is the only time she will sit still for fifty-two minutes at a stretch. While she communes with Oscar the Grouch and Big Bird, I slip little Greggie into his motorized swing and a Pilates videotape into the VCR. When I was single, I prided myself on not having a TV in my living room. Living rooms are for entertaining, not vegetating, or so I believed in that former life. Now I have two television sets in my living room—and I'd kill to vegetate. I make it halfway through my abdominal stretches and leg lifts before the swing stops and little Greggie begins to cry. I try to settle him down by starting up the swing again, but he's hungry. Again.

10:00 A.M.

Time for snack. I lift Alexis into the high chair and load the tray with bits of cheese and pretzel fish. I pack little Greggie into the baby sack and sling it around my neck. Hands free, I dial the pediatrician's office and ask to speak to the nurse. After eleven bits of cheese, twelve pretzel fish, and thirteen minutes on hold, the nurse finally comes on the line.

"What seems to be the problem, Mrs. Fink?"

Under my breath, I curse my husband and his silly surname. Aloud I say, "Little Greggie is always hungry."

"Then feed him, Mrs. Fink."

"He's nursing every couple of hours. He's always hungry. It's, uh . . ."—I struggle to find the right word—". . . relentless."

"I see."

"My nipples are torn up." I hope I don't sound as desperate as I feel.

There's a short pause. "I see here from your chart that your last time in the doctor gave you some cream for your nipples."

"It's not working. They're actually bleeding a little bit." I know I don't sound as desperate as I feel.

"Well, Mrs. Fink, your son is five months old now. He's probably heading into his six-month growth spurt. You can always try supplementing breast milk with formula until he gets through this phase."

I am determined to breastfeed little Greggie through the six-month mark, as I did his sister. "I didn't really want to do that."

"Entirely up to you, Mrs. Fink. We'll see you and the baby next month on the sixth for his checkup."

Dismissed.

Noon

My husband Mark will be home in six hours. I am giddy at the thought of adult conversation, flirtation, even—dare I say it—fornication. He's been gone two weeks, and although we've only had sex maybe three times since the baby was born, and then I was half asleep, now I actually find myself wide awake and aroused at the thought of it.

Little Greggie is in his playpen, batting at his Bob the Builder mobile. Alexis is helping me make sugar cookies. While she cheerfully dumps rainbow-colored sprinkles on the round slices of dough, I eye the Pillsbury roll with lust in my heart. Six hours. I need to take a bath. I can't remember the last time I bathed—was it yesterday or the day before?

2:00 P.M.

At long last, nap time! On good days, it's the only time during the day when both children are asleep, the only time during the day when I can take a bath, the only time of day when I can finish a complete thought in my head. On bad days, I go dirty.

Not taking any chances, I nurse the baby and then follow up with six ounces of formula. He finishes off both my breasts and the bottle in no time and nods off immediately. I slip him into his crib and shut the nursery door behind me. One down, one to go.

Alexis is in her room, lining up her stuffed animals on her little twin bed. She has several dozen by now—bears and lambs and puppies and kitties and bunnies and ponies and monkeys and even a couple of alligators and dinosaurs. She loves them all.

"Hi, Mommy."

"Time for your nap."

"Naps are for babies."

"Yes, that's true, but naps are for big girls, too."

Alexis stares at me with her father's gray eyes and says again, "Naps are for babies."

I really want that bath. "Big girls take naps, too. Now, into bed with all your critters." I use my "serious Mommy" voice.

Alexis doesn't budge. "Naps are for babies."

"I'm a big girl, and I take naps." I realize my mistake as soon as the words are out of my mouth.

Alexis hops into her bed, scattering stuffed animals. "Lay down with me, Mommy, and we'll take a Big Girl nap together." She smiles, a big dimpled smile, and I am charmed. I lie down with her, vowing to get up and take my bath as soon as she's asleep. But I doze off first.

4:00 P.M.

I wake up to the sound of Alexis giggling. She has buried me in stuffed animals. I laugh, buoyed by the unexpected beauty sleep, and pile critters on top of her in turn. This playtime continues until I realize that it is once again time for *Sesame Street*. I bundle up Alexis with her blankie and a dinosaur in front of the TV and survey the home my husband will waltz into fresh from le Champs-Elysees in Paris in just 120 minutes. It's no Versailles, even on a good day. And this is not a good day.

An hour and forty-five minutes later, the toys are in the toy chest, the dishes are in the dishwasher, and the dirty clothes are in the laundry room. *Sesame Street* is long over, so while I vacuum, Alexis runs the feather duster along the few surfaces she can reach. Little Greggie, miracle of miracles, is still asleep. It must be the formula. I can hardly believe my luck. I'll just have time for a quick bath and then . . . the baby monitor announces little Greggie with a characteristic shriek.

"Honey, I'm home!" Mark bounds in with a flourish, handsome and happy and smart enough to come bearing gifts. Alexis runs to him, and he presents her with a stuffed French poodle and then hugs them both. I get a French kiss and a quick feel and a shiny bag filled with what better be Chanel perfume and Simone Perele lingerie.

6:00 P.M.

I take the bag and head for little Greggie's room. I can remember when it was I returning from business trips to Paris, when it was I bearing luxury gifts from duty-free shops at international airports, when it was I who was greeted as the archetypal hero returning with the golden elixir. It wasn't that long ago— back before babies when I used to be a shower person, too.

I scoop up little Greggie and take him to the kitchen, where I pop a bottle of formula into the microwave to heat it up. Seconds later I return to my husband, hand him the baby and the bottle, and say, "I'm taking a bath."

"Okay." He smiles at me.

"I may be awhile."

"Take your time, honey."

8:00 P.M.

Like Venus, I emerge from the waters a new woman. Wrinkled, but new. I slip into the champagne-colored silk peignoir Mark has brought me and dab Chanel #5 perfume on my neck. The babies are sleeping. Mark is in our bed, reading the *Wall Street Journal.*

"That was a long bath," he says. I slide under the covers next to him. He looks at me as if he's not sure who I am.

"You used to take showers. Fast showers. Now you take these long baths. . . ."

"Baths are good for thinking." I kissed him. "And I've been thinking, now that little Greggie is on formula, I'd like to get a sitter three mornings a week. Do a little freelancing. You know, just to keep my hand in."

Mark smiles. "Sounds good." He reaches over to my grandmother's antique dresser and turns off the baby monitor.

With any luck, we've got till midnight.

It's not what I do, it's the way I do it.
It's not what I say, it's the way I say it.

Mae West

A writer, editor, and novelist, Paula Munier is the mother of three—Alexis, Gregory, and Mikey. She lives in rural Massachusetts in a lakeside cottage with her family, two dogs, and a cat.

What was the hardest part of that time you wrote about in this story?

The hardest part was the sleep deprivation. Having two babies so close together means you really don't get any sleep at all for about five years. Then, if you're as masochistic as I am, as soon as they're in school and you can finally catch up on your sleep, you have a third child. Before I had kids, I had hobbies like skiing and museum touring. Once I had kids, sleep became my hobby.

What has happened since this story was written?

I had a third child and went back to work.

How was the third child different?

By the third child, you're a lot smarter—or maybe you're just tired. With my first two children, I was overzealous. I only let them watch PBS; I only gave them frozen yogurt and home-made popcorn for dessert; I only let my mother baby-sit. I spent all day every day reading to them, running in the park with them, making arts and crafts with them. I thought that my superior parenting skills were the reason that they were so bright and wonderful. With the third child, all of that changed. Mikey went into day care full-time at seven months, eats M&M's for breakfast, and watches Cartoon Network twenty-four hours a day. Yet, so far, he's as smart and wonderful as his siblings. Go figure.

How did you feel going back to work?
It was fabulous—and terrible. I was torn. I'm still torn. On the plus side, I feel like a real grownup again. My gray cells are back in high gear. I love the social interaction, the intellectual stimulation, the company of my peers . . . oh, and the high heels. I love dressing up and going out somewhere every day. On the negative side, I loved being home with the kids. I try to spend as much time with them as I can—but it's never enough.

Have you been back to Paris?
Last year, we spent a week in April in Paris—all of us. The children, who'd never been there before, fell in love with the city, as I had done many years before. Paris is as glorious as ever, even more beautiful than I remember.

Do you still consider yourself a bath person?
Now that I'm back at work full-time, I'm a grooming schizophrenic. On weekdays, I take very short showers; on weekends, I indulge myself in long, long, long baths.

Lifeline

❀

Laurie Elmquist

The day I sat down with my bank manager, I didn't have a specific house in mind; I just wanted to know, was I in the ballpark? The manager, who looked to be about my age, in his early thirties, was something of a celebrity. He was going to be on *Who Wants to Be a Millionaire?* the all-Canadian version. He was just waiting for the call to fly to New York.

"Let's take a look," he said, turning to his computer screen, where he had access to all my vital statistics, my checking and savings, and what I had stashed in my retirement account.

"I'm looking in Fairfield," I said. I'd moved to Victoria five years ago, and it hadn't taken me long to fall in love with this neighborhood of artists and potters and funky houses in purples and blues. I'd rented a house across from a park, but now the house was slated for demolition.

The manager punched a few more keys. He wore a gold wedding band with a single diamond in the center. On the wall behind him was a photo of a blond woman, his wife, I guessed, with a little towheaded boy on her lap.

"I'll need a letter of employment," he said, folding his hands in front of him.

He would be good on set. I could see him deliberating each question, respectful of the procedure, no matter how inane the choices. He might even call the host by her first name. *That's my final answer, Pamela.*

"It's standard procedure," he continued. "Years of employment. Salary."

"I've been with the college five years." I didn't tell him that I was a term instructor, still waiting to be hired into a full-time position.

"Houses are pricey in Fairfield," he said. "My wife and I started looking there, but then we bought in Gordon Head."

"I have my heart set on Fairfield." As soon as I said "heart," I wished I could take it back. Bank managers dealt with numbers, not feelings.

He arranged the papers on his desk. "Once I have the letter, I'll be able to give you a better idea of what you can expect." He held out his hand to conclude our meeting.

I felt like an actor—thumbs down at the first audition.

Driving home, I thought about all the reasons I wanted to buy a house. I wanted something solid and permanent. My life was full of transients—students who passed through my classes on their way to earning a degree, and housemates who intended to go on to study law in Toronto or save turtles in Costa Rica. In the evening, I took my stack of grading to a coffee shop, finding company in the hubbub of voices.

The next day, I told my creative writing students I was trying to buy a house, and they looked at me skeptically. How could someone who was buying a house teach them anything about anarchy? But these days, I didn't feel like tearing things down. All around me, my friends were getting married, having babies, and putting down roots. I wanted something substantial to show the world in the same way you could hold a baby up and say, *Look at this.* I wanted my friends and family to send cards that said, *Congratulations on your new home.*

Lately, I'd been feeling like I hadn't done much in my thirty-two years, except go to school. But the letter of employment from the college surprised me, the way resumes sometimes do by making you look like you've actually accomplished something in life. Julie, in human resources, had done it up on official letterhead. It stated how long I'd been teaching and how much I made. It didn't say anything about whether I was a term employee or full-time instructor. Bless her heart.

The bank manager wasn't there when I dropped it off, but I gave it to one of the women who worked behind the scenes in a small glass cubicle.

When I got home, I took my dog out for a walk around the block. On the next street over, I found a For Sale sign that hadn't been there the day before. It was a Tudor-style house with leaded windowpanes and a front lawn that was all rocks and tulips. According to the information sheet in a pouch below the For Sale sign, it was a two-bedroom house built in 1912. It had a finished basement with a one-bedroom suite, something I could rent out to help pay the mortgage. My stomach muscles tightened. This could be the one.

On Saturday, I arrived at the Open House before anyone else, including the agent who was showing it. I sat down on the bottom step in the sunlight, watching the wrens flit in the camellia bush. The agent arrived a few minutes later, apologizing because she was late.

The house was tiny; it was like stepping into a cottage, except with very high ceilings. Everything was painted white, the walls, the century-old trim, and the mantel. The only deviation was a hearth of blood-red tiles. I could imagine a lot more color in this room, perhaps a red couch. I looked under the beige broadloom to see the oak flooring beneath. "Oak in the front room," the agent said. "Fir in the dining room. That's the way they did it back then."

I'd lived in enough rentals to know the difference between a house whose sole purpose was to earn income and one that had been cared for, in this case by the same woman for over twenty-five years. "She raised her daughter here," the agent said, leading me into the kitchen, "but now her daughter's away at university." Everywhere was new cabinetry and countertops and drawers that slid like butter on their tracks. "Handy to have a pots and pans drawer," the agent said.

I felt like I was entering a world that might be easier than the one I had lived in. Here, the sink was white instead of stainless steel. Here was a dining room where you could put an oak table, cover it with a tablecloth, and put a vase of tulips in the middle, just like you saw in magazines. Here was a living room that invited a plush, new sofa, not one that was rescued off the curb. In this house, I could see my life changing into something softer, more beautiful.

When I returned home and called my real estate agent, he suggested offering the full price.

"Aren't you supposed to get me a deal?" I asked.

"There's no room to bargain on this one," he said. "It's Fairfield."

I hesitated.

"It would be even stronger if we could go in a little over the asking price," he said.

Within an hour, my offer was accepted. Subject to a building inspection and financing, I had myself a house with all the appliances, everything I'd asked for except the bird bath. *Hallelujah!*

When I called the bank on Monday, they told me the manager was back and could see me later that day. I'd heard he'd made it to $250,000 with the help of his lifeline. In a radio interview with the *Ocean*, he said he was going to pay off the mortgage on his house and take his wife and son to Disneyland.

I laid the file on his desk. "That's the one," I said, showing him the picture. "That's the house I have to have."

He scanned the information.

"Ever have that gut instinct where you just know?" I asked.

He looked at me through oval steel-rimmed glasses, "Gut instinct is one thing, but it's my job to make sure the numbers add up."

"Yes, the numbers."

"A bigger down payment would help."

"There's a suite in the basement," I said. "The woman who owns the house says she's getting six hundred dollars a month."

"Says nothing here about a *legal* suite. The City could shut you down at any time. If there was someone else," he said, "someone else on title. Two incomes are always better."

"I'm alone on this one." I folded my hands in front of me. I knew it was a lot of money to ask for. I knew it was a stretch and that everything I had in savings would go into this first home. I knew it would be easier if I had someone behind me in a framed photograph, like he did.

"It would help if we closed out your credit cards," he said.

"Do what you have to do."

The building inspector was a short, muscular man with curly hair and an Irish accent. We met at the house on a sunny afternoon.

"Sometimes, you just know it's right," I said, walking into the living room. The sunlight bounced off a prism that hung in the front window, creating a rainbow on the opposite wall.

He consulted his clipboard. "The fireplace will never work."

"How about a pressed log?"

He shook his head.

"A candle?"

He led me outside to the backyard. "Don't get too attached to that apple tree." It was in full bloom, the pink blossoms swarming with bees and filling the yard with a sweet fragrance. "It's got maybe two summers in it, which is more than I can say for this flat roof." He pointed to the roof over the back bedroom. "It needs replacing immediately."

He tried to show me the age of the house, windows that would never open, a porch badly in need of repair. I wasn't so completely love-struck that I couldn't see the house needed some work, but I was already thinking about new planks and replacement windows and calculating how I would pay for it. *How much for a flat roof?*

In the bank manager's office, I sat nervously, waiting for the financing to be completed.

"You forgot to sign here," he said. I was sure he would find me out. Someone would run in at the last minute and tell him that I didn't have a permanent contract at the college and therefore was too great a risk. And then, the landlord would tell me that the City had approved his plans, and I would have to move. Again.

"Here," he said, pushing the contract toward me. "You *do* want the house?"

The house, I wanted, but not the figures on the sheet in front of me. I owed $225,000. It was unfathomable.

He must have seen the terror in my face. He pointed out a few good things in the shuffle of paper. The low taxes, for one. Although there was a good chance they'd go up once the house was reassessed. The low interest rate, another. On the day I signed my mortgage, it was 4.7 percent. There was a time when it was 21 percent. "*Twenty-one,*" he emphasized.

My stomach lurched.

At the lawyer's, I wrote a check for $39,499.59.

The woman who took it reminded me of my grandmother. I wanted to tell her about the house, about the bundles of tea towels I had purchased, the chenille pillow covers, the wooden picture frames for the mantel. I wanted to tell her that my grandmother once worked for a lawyer, too. There was no time. She pressed a photocopy of the check into my hand. "This is for your scrapbook," she said.

Then I was in the elevator because the office of Hunt & Cooper bred briskness. As I rode down to the first floor, I said to myself, *You just bought yourself a house.*

And then, in the mirrored reflection, *Good for you.*

I wanted to live. I wanted
to live in a house where the door
swings on hinges smooth as the sea.

Lorna Crozier

Laurie Elmquist has had short stories published in Prairie Fire *and the anthology* Wrestling with the Angel *(Red Deer Press, 2000). She is currently working on a collection of linked stories entitled* How Are Things in Lotus Land? *She holds an MA in English Literature and Creative Writing from the University of Windsor and lives in Victoria, British Columbia, where she teaches creative writing and Canadian literature at Camosun College.*

Was home ownership everything you dreamed it would be?

For four years, I owned my own home, and it was the best decision I ever made. I painted the walls of my study yellow. I tore out the shag rug in the back bedroom and had the hardwood flooring refinished. I planted rosebushes in the front yard and an herb garden in the back. I got to know my neighbors because I planned on being there forever.

How did the renovations go?
The building inspector was right about everything. The apple tree died the second summer I was there and had to be cut down. The chimney was inoperable. At night, I'd lie awake worrying about the flat roof. Finally, I had enough savings to call the roofers. I always thought you had to be a handyman to own a house, but it's not true. You just have to be able to pay the handyman.

Were you able to rent out the downstairs unit?
Yes. Thank goodness for tenants. If it weren't for them, I don't know how I would have paid the mortgage and ever-rising property taxes. For the first two years, one of my closest friends lived in the suite in the basement. I'd call down when dinner was ready or he'd call up. He was the better cook, but I had the bigger living room and the more comfortable couch. While we ate dinner, we'd watch *Blind Date* together and dream of a time when we wouldn't be single.

Do you still live in the house?
In my third summer of living in the house, a Californian with beautiful hazel eyes bought the house across the street from me. I gave him a sunflower plant, a small housewarming gift. Six months later, he asked me to marry him. I said, yes. We decided

to sell both our houses and buy a new one together. We found a two-story house in the same neighborhood, also built in 1912, but with a view of the ocean.

What advice do you have for first-time homebuyers?
Jump in. Leap. It's a little like falling in love.

Josephine's Tattoo

Josephine Rich

It was the predictability that was suffocating me. Every morning, I felt myself being sucked under the current of petty domestic chores and child care, like being pinned helplessly in the tumbling momentum of the surf, never knowing when the inevitable revolutions might throw me up for a snatch of air.

Every day seemed the same. The washing machine would beep the end of its spin cycle, and I'd tug the wet clothes into a plastic basket, pick my way through the backyard debris of deflated balls, rusting bicycles, and abandoned sweaters to the line. Some days, I imagined I'd performed exactly the same chore, made exactly the same movement, even sighed or yawned at the same second as I had on a previous day, and my body felt limp with desperation.

Some days in the supermarket, gasping in the plastic fragrance of the laundry and cleaning aisles, I toyed with trivial whims. I would shave my head or get a nipple pierced. I would score some dope, make cookies with it, and then offer them round with the coffee at my next Mothers' Meeting. I would approach the next man who smiled at me and give him unconditional sex in the back of his car. Instead, I'd go home and dig in the garden, my heart easing as I felt the sweat collect in the small of my back. And then it would be time for the school run, and I'd be treading water again.

Jack was away most of the time. Two- or three-month contracts on a rig in the South China Sea. We had met in Asia. I'd had a good corporate job in Singapore and was living an expatriate life of excess: working too hard, drinking too much, too busy for relationships, too lonely to feel fulfilled. Girls like me didn't look at *rig pigs*. There were four or five of them at the bar that night, fingering the cash in their pockets, buying drinks for willowy Asian beauties, laughing too loud. His arms resting on the bar mesmerized me. I let them seduce me.

The next morning, I told him that he was to leave, that it had been fun, but better left uncomplicated by identities, histories, futures. He stayed for two weeks, laying siege to my house, changing its smell and space, spreading himself through my ordered life until it was no longer my own. Six years later, I had two children, a dog, and a dream house in a respectable but faceless middle-class suburb. Sometimes I struggled to remember how I got there, like I had woken up in someone else's life by mistake.

By the time Robbie and Cat were at school, Jack's home leave seemed to have become shorter, reeking of duty rather than desire. In bed, his wiry body was a foreign country. The smell of other women seeped through his pores, like someone else's cooking in my kitchen. I didn't have the courage to confront my intuition. Instead, I hung it out to dry with the sheets or tucked it under the collars of the children's uniforms as I ironed.

And then Sam came.

At first, there was only the dull thud of music next door, movements of garbage bins and car doors shutting in the early hours of the morning. Then, one afternoon, digging at the back of the garden, I became conscious of my own movements and, looking up, saw a square face perched on the lip of the fence, the budding beginnings of blonde dreadlocks scooped into a black band, a cleft in the chin accentuated as the jaw rested on the unsanded wood. "Are you digging your way out? The Great Escape?" The voice was relaxed, the tone unusually rich and soft.

"Huh. Very funny," I breathed, wiping my face on my sleeve.

"Only kidding. It must be tough doing it all on your own— the single mom thing."

"I'm not on my own. I'm married." I didn't know whether to feel disturbed or flattered that someone had noticed.

"Not around much, though, is he?"

"No. You've been doing your homework."

There was a pause as the dreadlocks were untied and rescooped back into the black band. "Shall we start again? Hello, I'm Sam, house-sitter for David next door, itinerant bartender, struggling artist, tactless, curious, annoying. I think that about sums it up."

A lean hand was proffered over the fence, and I shook it, lethargically offering:

"Hello, I'm Jo. Housewife. Mother. I think that about sums it up."

"Oh, does it?" A thick blonde eyebrow rose briefly, and I noticed steady blue eyes, more confident than my own, though easily ten years younger. "So, white and one for me," Sam threw over the fence, and I saw the dreadlocks drifting along it to the front of the house.

"Oh, um, coffee or tea?"

I heard the panic in my own voice. I didn't socialize with people much, in fact, nothing beyond playground meetings with other mothers: predictable, claustrophobic, but strangely comforting in their mix of cappuccinos, cake, and unchallenging conversation. Now there would be a stranger in my kitchen, someone not of my kind. I would have to think, appear charming, be judged. As I ran back to the house and kicked off my boots, I realized that I would have to resurrect my childless identity, and I was almost paralyzed by the sudden fear that it might no longer exist.

"So what did you do before all this? Before the suburban thing?" Sam was lounging on one of my barstools at the kitchen counter, in jeans and a cotton shirt splattered with paint, one buttock propped on the rattan of the seat, one long leg stretched out into the center of the kitchen. I had to keep stepping over a bare foot to make the coffee, but rather than move it, Sam seemed to take amusement from its inconvenience.

"I was in banking in Asia."

"And before that?"

"In banking in London."

"And before that?"

"At college."

"Not Finance, no." Sam gave an elaborate shudder.

"No, Medieval and Early Renaissance Literature actually."

"There! I knew it. I knew there had to be some secret passion."

"What, poring over dusty manuscripts in Cambridge to write a thesis that no one will ever read about books that no one ever reads? Maybe I did have a passion, but I was young and didn't know much else, apart from academia."

"So how did you get from the Middle Ages to money markets and flannel suits?"

"Oh, I guess life gets in the way. Passion gives way to the practicalities of living." I thought of Jack entwined with a Malay girl while I passionately took a plunger to the kitchen sink for the tenth time that week or caught the naked moonlit reflection of myself in the mirror as I took Cat to pee in the middle of the night.

"Is painting your passion then?" I spoke into the door of the fridge, attempting to tack away from myself.

"Mm, among other things."

When I swung around, I found myself confronted with a naked back, square at the shoulders and tapering smoothly to the waist, covered almost entirely with tattoos in minute detail: a woman's eye, lovers with arms and legs entwined, the frond of a fern about to spring open, a wave breaking. It could so easily have been cheap and raw, but the artwork was exceptional and the shape of the back itself made me want to glide my hands down its flanks and feel it under my breasts. I was left groping for words.

"I designed most of them." Sam was buttoning up. "I've sold a few designs, but it doesn't pay the rent. I do a few murals, tend bar, house-sit. Life is pretty good, I guess." And then, almost without drawing breath, "Let me draw you."

I was floundering again, and to regain some sense of control, I tried to condescend with the superiority of age. "Yeah, right. *Study of an Aging Housewife*, really interesting. Anyway, probably couldn't sit still for more than five minutes."

"No, seriously. When you dig your garden, I like to see the curve of the vertebrae under your T-shirt and the shape of the sweat seeping between your shoulders. Your body works. It would be a good study."

I turned away toward the kettle and tried to let go of the knot at the base of my neck.

• • •

Sam stood at an easel behind a large plywood board marked on the reverse side with erratic strokes in charcoal and the remnants of masking tape from previous sketches. I felt oddly annoyed at the idea of other women in front of the easel, and then the annoyance itself annoyed me.

"Right, get your clothes off, then." Sam's voice came from behind the easel.

I went over to a wicker chair and sat on it to undo my sneakers and wriggle off my jeans and underpants, confronting the awkward vulnerability I've always felt at doctors' physicals. Being nude in broad daylight in front of a clothed person made me feel large and disjointed, cartoonlike. I was still turning the feeling over when I felt a hand on my hip and another over the nape of my neck. Sam's palms were cool and dry and moved me confidently, thumbs pressing into my skin like a sculptor's on clay.

"I want you to have your back to me and lean slightly—"

I began to stop listening and follow only the pressure of the hands. It had been a long time. I noticed the hairs on my arms were raised and the skin around my nipples had filled out.

There were no words exchanged as Sam drew. The spin, the humor were gone. The room became heavy with breath, with the hollow scratch of charcoal on paper, the tearing of new sheets and masking tape. I became intensely aware of every sound, of my own shape, each hair, my pulse, the rise of my ribs for air. Eventually, I felt exhausted by it, like laboring with a child. Every so often, I felt the sudden cool stroke of Sam's palm over a shoulder blade, my triceps, a hamstring, as if the touch was needed to translate my body to the paper.

Finally, I heard tape being pulled off the board and watched as a sheet, tossed into the air, floated to the floorboards.

"I'm done. They're all right for a first go, but I didn't quite crack you." Sam came up behind me as I was dressing and kissed between my bare shoulders. "Thanks for being so still—and patient."

I virtually ran home, not stopping to look at the sketches, leaving some excuse trailing behind me about getting back for the baby-sitter. The kiss was still heavy between my shoulders and had made me wet. I felt like a schoolgirl and was angry with myself.

I slid beneath the surface of the bath water and held the breath in my cheeks. Sam was playing me for fun, a small project to while away the time. But, then, did it really matter? It was trivial in the grand scheme of things, and wasn't it what I needed? There was no great scandal, not by today's standards. A brief affair, something simple, instinctive, unexplored. I was finding my childless self again. I was coming up for air in the suffocating swell of the past seven years.

Dripping onto the carpet as I picked up the receiver of the phone, I stalled briefly as I heard Sam's voice answer, lazy from sleep. Then I filled my lungs with air and said slowly, "It's me, Jo. Can you come over? The door's unlocked."

There were many more tattoos that I discovered, studying each new find, watching it move over muscle, admiring its starkness outlined against the white of my sheets or wrapped around the comparative paleness of my own skin. Strangely, someone so distinct from Jack, so removed, made me think of him more. It wasn't guilt or vengeance, but purely practical consideration: I had suddenly begun to think about how I felt to him when he made love to me, what the fleshy curve of my breasts or the arch of my back meant, the taste, the sound of myself.

One morning, Sam was gone. There were twelve nudes in charcoal rolled up on my doorstep and another small sketch that I had never seen before with a brief note, "Come up for air sometimes. Love, Sam."

Jack arrived home three weeks later. I found suddenly that I had an urgent desire to spread my smell over him, reclaim him.

"You look well, Jo, kind of rested," he said, as he brushed his brown fingers through the strands of my hair laid out on the pillow.

"Mm, I feel good," I murmured, turning my back into him.

He brushed the hair from the base of my neck, moving as if to kiss it, then pulled his head away abruptly. I felt him run his forefinger over the intricate tattoo of a mermaid in miniature, bursting through water, her torso bare and expanded in breath, head tilted upwards and eyes half closed.

"Why—when did you get this done?"

I smiled at his trying not to sound shocked. "David's housesitter designed it for me. I got it done a few weeks ago. Spur of the moment. I used to do things like that, remember?"

He smoothed the tattoo with two fingers. "It's very good. It's really quite beautiful. He was a good artist, then, this housesitter of David's?"

"She was. She was a very good artist," I replied. I closed my eyes and saw the outline of myself on white paper.

Life forms illogical patterns.
It is haphazard and full of beauties
which I try to catch as they fly by,
for who knows whether any of them will ever return.

Margot Fonteyn

Josephine Rich was born and raised in Northamptonshire, England, virtually next door to Princess Diana. She has herself been referred to as a "princess" on many occasions, but the similarities end there. She spent the first part of her life looking for sunshine in England, but now spends her days searching for shade in Australia, where she now lives with her partner and two children. She is researching stories of how childbirth can empower women to realize their full potential. She believes that, for women today, becoming a mother poses one of the greatest challenges. If they can survive childbirth and child rearing, they can handle pretty much everything.

Did you ever tell your husband about Sam?

No, I never told Jack, and I probably never will. I mean, the whole experience with Sam was not about my relationship with Jack; it was not about jealousy or getting even with him because of his affairs. It was about me, about rediscovering a little something of myself again after years of being a wife and mother. If I told Jack about it, he would want to know intricate details (wouldn't most men?), and I think that would end up being destructive for both of us. Why dissect something that has brought us closer than we've been in years? And don't think that I'm being hypocritical—I never have tried to grill Jack about his past affairs. I just don't want to go there. Maybe I'm a coward, but don't you think that sometimes we can be really self-destructive in our thirst for details, for the absolute truth? For me, the end justifies the means.

How did this interlude with Sam change your life?

Did it change my life? Absolutely. Perhaps not on the outside (except for my little souvenir—the tattoo), but on the inside it was liberating, a big, huge breath of fresh air. I needed to mentally shrug off that stale coat of marriage and mothering for a while to be able to see what I had become. "Boring" and "bored" spring to mind. As much as I wanted to blame Jack for playing around, I realized I'd let myself fall into this rut of suburban routine. I needed someone like Sam to help shake me up, to question things and, along the way, to give me back something of my own identity: the challenging, thinking person I used to be. Being able to see myself again has let me become more inspired in the way I am with the kids and with Jack.

How did the affair affect your relationship with your husband?

Look, I'm not saying that going out and having an affair has suddenly been the answer to all our marital problems, but it has certainly spiced things up. I know now how much I actually value Jack. I know that I love making love to him, and I know all this because I know a bit more about myself.

Have you ever heard back from Sam?

No. And I wouldn't expect to. It was kind of an unspoken agreement—a classic case of less being more. And I wouldn't go out looking for more of the same. It was a moment in time. One of the good ones that you snatch before it passes you by and then you savor because you know it's not going to happen again.

I Do and the All-Male Revue

Allison Kornet

Last weekend, a dear friend with a classic bearing and benign tastes came to Boston for her bachelorette party. In three weeks, Becca will marry a forty-one-year-old American Airlines pilot, move with him and his aging dog into a fixer-upper townhouse by the river, dream of maternity leave and strollers, and sink ever more cozily into the Talbots' red-door demographic. There would be no bras on her head at the bachelorette party, no games about exes or embarrassing props to cart around town as the girl bevy got sloshed.

"What do you want to do?" I asked.

"Something fun," she said. "A spa day maybe. Or the symphony."

So I opened the paper, found the ad, and bought us all tickets to Chippendales. Chippendales, the all-male dance revue—not animated chipmunks making mischief in tree limbs, but live, lithe men built like tractors and plowing the stage in various states of deshabille.

Like my upstanding pal Becca and the rest of her upstanding gal pals, I had never been to Chippendales and knew I'd probably never go unless someone like me enforced the experience. You can't poll your friends and give them a chance to get anxious and hypothetical. You have to assess the situation, assume the proper state of mind, commit, and take whatever happens for the team. Sort of like saying "I do."

Or saying "I do" Becca-style. My friend—the girl who was thirteen with me, shared cookies and the curling iron, even went for similar guys once upon a time—was now signing up for something "I" would never "do." Her choice of future and fiancé felt extreme, disappointing even. We were supposed to be adventurers, women of the world. We were supposed to be the ones flying the planes, not marrying the pilots and waiting on or for them at home.

"You're in for a surprise," I told Becca. "Stick with me."

I had to be equally murky in e-mails to the others, for fear defectors would kill the festivities. *We're going to a show,* I wrote. *From the producer of N-SYNC and the Backstreet Boys.* This wasn't the respectability I was going for, but it was the truth, and good enough. The others may have suspected what was up. But they could say they didn't, and that was all they needed.

The Chippendales were a no-lose situation. If we encountered unconscionable raunch, we'd laugh about it and give Becca one more reason to move along into her next chapter. If we encountered something else—something strong and lively, say, or compellingly *hard*—well, maybe something else was in order for our futures.

Let me declare outright that I loved the show. They had me at hello, the very moment the lights were searching the stage for the missing men, and in the darkness of the last row with my calves pressed against the lip of my bar stool, heels locked as I balanced on its rung, I felt them brush past me in one striding line of virility. There were three or four of them on my side, and they all wore black Matrix trench coats that skated out behind them as they made for the stage to meet up with the others. They felt tall and mysterious, and when they turned from the flanks to face us and lock into place, they stayed that way. Had they pulled off those Matrix layers and begun writhing mindlessly about the platform, slick would have quickly turned to slime. But they did something much better. They danced. Hard.

A platoon of eight or ten guys matched each other limb for limb in vigorous maneuvers, angles aggressive, voltage high. These were no party-boy antics, no beer-in-one-hand, look-at-my-groove let-me-feature-this-move batch of dance-floor affectations. These were drills, this was sweat, all of it was timing, and over two hours the impression the men sustained was one of symmetry, collaboration, power. I found it impossible to watch and not imagine the studio time, the sessions of training such a performance must have required. Yeah, I found it sexy. Talent is always sexy. So are bronzed lats engaged in rhythmic, one-armed pushups. So is a rack of abs stretched out for a handspring. So are quads you could drive a train over. So is skin.

Becca was giggling. And beside her, Kristen, a married mom-in-the-works, was peeling bills from her pocket and handing them over to our bride-to-be shamelessly, in case the action moved closer. Beside them danced the rest of our petite entourage, hips swaying, wrists casually airborne and twirling. Beside *them*, I was philosophizing on art and action. In other words, I was gawking.

When a bare-torsoed, bow-tied bar boy shifted toward me for a drink order, I shook a "no thank you" at his paneled parts and had the distinct impression he would balance better if turned upside down and allowed to walk on his hands.

If I had a boyfriend (I hadn't for months) and if he were sitting home in a leather chair reading the newspaper on this Friday evening (he wouldn't be), if I arrived back all flushed from my girls' night out (I would), and if said boyfriend were suddenly wearing a cardigan, turning to me kindly, and asking (as Becca's man might) how I had found the show, what would I say?

First, I'd ask how I wound up dating Fred Rogers.

Then maybe I'd get technical, tell him male dance was a form of expression, a spirited communication demanding discipline and skill. Anything to disguise the fact that I'd just been to a glorified striptease, the stage where grown men play dress-up and reenact what someone has told them are typical female fantasies: officers in dress whites, marching super-slow-mo and saluting to an invisible authority; bachelors dreaming at home alone, hugging pillows and casting about in pristine PJs. It was ludicrous.

Granted, it doesn't take much to bumble around in bedroom duds with the body God gave you. This is something my mother would have said in the years before she decided to become sensitive to "my situation"—the situation of being a single woman in her thirties.

When my mother was my age, she'd already had me, and I was her third. How could she know what it was like to go indefinitely long without the excitement, the comfort, the consistency of intimacy? My lovely, modest mother, who "waited" for engagement to my more experienced dad before "giving the gift." Who urged me to wait for "the one."

Well, I was waiting, in my way, and what I'd encountered so far was a series of little losses. Guys I loved would choose someone or something I wouldn't, and the horizon would rise up between us. Then, worse, girlfriends would do the same. They'd make a plan or form a pair, and then they too would recede, it seemed, into the curve of the earth.

Beside me and my path there was Becca and hers, and for a moment at the club, I felt the four of us surveying the scene. We watched the Chippendales bend at the waist, flex their hamstrings and glutes, and in perfect pike positions, all upside down and playful, ask, quite literally, *Are you ready to leave this behind?*

When between acts a lecherous emcee called, "Is there one horny woman in the room, just one?" cheese practically dripping from his chops, many more than one woman squealed pitiably, predictably, in reply, and it was impossible for our group not to look at each other and grimace. *Whoa, now. Don't turn that spotlight on us. We're just here spectating, having a time. We're backing away from the boys with our hands up.*

Even the attributes of the tallest, darkest, indisputably super-est stud of all stretched toward the grotesque once he ripped off his Oxford and revealed a tight little Superman T, too small even for his air of vanity. He was handsome, all right, striking for both feat and features, but he made Becca grimace and had a similar effect on me, safe in the anonymity of our back row.

"Put your clothes back on!" I hollered. He was not somebody a person could live with.

In the whole Chippendales lot, in fact, only one guy accommodated the fantasy of compatibility. Detecting him halfway through the show, Becca and I began to call him "Boy Next Door," and he broke our candy hearts. He was relaxed and warm and smiled authentically as he hit the stances for fun, as if despite himself. He seemed to be joy personified, and when Kristen called him over to Becca, a former school admissions officer, a woman who works with *people,* he looked her in the eye and neither of them could keep up the conceit.

"You having a good time?" he said, as though tending to his sister at commencement.

I could have swiped her dollar while they had this little human exchange, could have slid it right up the boardwalk of his beautiful thigh, but the very person-ness of Boy Next Door simply did not permit. The guy could not be objectified. He was the best sort of tease: a tease for something deeper.

After that, the evening was over. On the way out, I asked Becca if she'd had a good time and if, all in all, she still wanted to get married.

"Of course," she said, loyalty flaring broadly in her grin.

When I saw it, something in me aligned. *She's not leaving her man,* I thought. And why did I finally get this? Because it was linked, of course, to the other thing her face made obvious: *She's not leaving me, either.*

I tossed my arm over Becca's shoulder, at last understanding what I'd hauled us off to the Roxie to see. Whatever our paths, my friend and I were committed—to each other, to our choices, to challenging and supporting each other as we made our choices. This was our common denominator across decades; so evident, I was embarrassed to have ever missed or doubted it.

Becca's good to go, I realized. *And so am I.* This was not my mother's thirty-one, but it was ours.

The clichés of a culture sometimes tell the deepest truths.

Faith Popcorn

Allison Kornet has worked as a newspaper and magazine editor, a high school English teacher, a team-building consultant, and a rowing coach. Nowadays, when she's not out on the river, she's shopping for agents to represent her first book, a collection of true stories and reflections about rounding age thirty with burglars, psychics, mortgage brokers, and singer-songwriters— all after the devastating loss of her older sister, Diana, who fell from the summit of Mt. Hood. Allison lives in Boston with her cat, Zoey, her dreams of warmer winters, and the rest of her family nearby.

Did you glean any other insights during the rest of the wedding festivities?

Well, I toasted Becca and her guy warmly at their wedding, and I meant every word. During that intense week of preparation and celebration, I got to know her groom better and see first-hand two important things: He loved the same woman I did, for many of the same reasons, and he respected our friendship as its own thing. So our relationship remains as it always was. We're both crazy busy and have to be persistent and patient about catching up with each other, but when we do, we still have that good connection.

Has your relationship with Becca changed since she married?

If anything, it's Becca's turn now to circle me and my choices. I've since met the man I hope to marry, a warm and lively co-adventurer, and I can't simply tell her, "We have the same birthday! He sings in the car! He likes my feet!" Becca will celebrate that stuff with me, yes, but I know she's also listening to see if I'm facing the tough issues: the fact that my guy has been married before, for example, and the fact that his family would prefer never to meet me. Becca knows the full story, and it's important she understand and support me as I grow with this other person.

Why doesn't his family want to meet you?

Because they're still coming to terms with his divorce. I think, for many families, divorce represents a kind of death and with it comes a very real grief that makes it hard to move on. There's a hole in the household; things feel fragmented; very specific expectations or dreams are disappointed. Who wants to embrace a new person when you're still mourning the loss of another?

So marriage is something you will contemplate, then?
Definitely. I'm actually a romantic when it comes to marriage. It's the flip side of being cynical about it—you only get suspicious that something will fall short when it matters very much to you that it doesn't. I don't want to be alone. I want to share all the good stuff. But I don't want to get a script, either.

Have you returned to Chippendales or to any other "all-male revue"?
I think one time was enough for me. On the one hand, you're caught up in this rare and tribal female experience where you're celebrating these fantastically fit men whose bodies are telling you at a primal level, Preservation of the species! Hope for the flowers! On the other, the experience is so embarrassing. To make reservations, you have to call the private cell line of this brazen-voiced, manhandling woman, and you can practically hear her judging how pathetic and unfulfilling your life is as she asks why you're late making reservations. You know she's off somewhere more glamorous, rifling through racks of gold halter tops and fluffy pink loungewear, a bodyguard named T-bone in tow . . . and that's just how you feel before you get to the show. When you get there, you're even embarrassed for the dancers. Do their mothers know they're here? You wonder. Do their girlfriends?

One Ring to Rule My Life

❧

Jill Patterson

On the caprock where we lived, my husband kept his eye, sharp as the West Texas sun, trained on me. At home, I couldn't grade papers, read a book, or paint my nails because my solitary activities excluded him. If I lunched with girlfriends from church or coworkers from the university, he wanted a transcript of our conversations. He couldn't believe I had time to play midday. Why wasn't I sharing the noon hour with him?

At night, slumber stole me away to another world, a galaxy cool and purple and moonlit, where his rules, like gravity, lost their grip. To keep me awake and aware of his presence, he kicked, stole my pillow, yanked the sheets. Sometimes his elbow jabbed the hollow of my eye; sometimes his hand smacked my cheek.

In the morning, I couldn't shower without him demanding admission to the bathroom. He needed the mirror, the toilet, to see me, naked, *now.* My showers only lasted fifteen minutes, but what if the warm spray of water on my skin—the luxury of solitude—encouraged me to daydream, to conjure lovers or forget the wedding band I removed when I bathed?

Three years after our vows, as I neared my thirty-fourth birthday, the prison routine had worn me down. I felt old, dead already, like a clunker abandoned in a pasture, stripped of its good parts. That weekend, my sister came to the caprock for spring shopping. She knew a wardrobe for summer weather would perk me up. She knew I needed dainty sandwiches from my favorite bakery, three hours in my favorite store, maybe a movie that evening. She knew she was the one person my husband would let me spend time with alone.

After our first day of shopping, we lay on the bed, pooped, fingering our purchases and laughing about who spent the least money for the most merchandise. I showed her a magazine picture of a shirt I'd bought that morning, though the shirt wasn't what I wanted.

"See how her belly's pierced?" I asked. "I want *that.*"

She stared at me. "You're teasing."

I looked over my shoulder, down the hallway, toward the living room where my husband was watching television. "We won't tell him yet. It'll be our secret."

"You're serious," she said. She knew I had to be to do anything without my husband's permission. I couldn't cut up a pan of brownies without asking him which knife to use, couldn't cut my hair without showing him sample styles, couldn't pack a suitcase without revealing what I'd loaded inside.

I shrugged. "I'll tell him you were the instigator."

We both smiled at the irony: The one person my husband trusted to baby-sit me was the person daring me to pierce my belly. Little did he know my sister had always coaxed me into doing crazy stunts. "Let's play cops and robbers," she would say when we were little girls. "You be the cop. I'll heist the bank. When I flee the scene astride my Harley, you yell, *Stop in the name of the law!*" Well, I yelled. She didn't stop. She rammed that bike between my legs, plowed me to the ground, and sped away with the Monopoly cash. Next, she'd say, "Let's play target practice." She propped me on a tricycle and commanded, "Pedal fast as you can, back and forth across the drive. And quack like a duck." When I shook my head no, she promised, "They're only BBs. They won't hurt."

"Okay," she said, looking at the magazine photo again. "Get the phone book."

The Yellow Pages listed two tattoo and body-piercing parlors. We scouted them and decided that the one next to the car stereo shop, not the one sandwiched between a drive-thru liquor store and the local strip joint, looked the most sanitary. We were in our thirties. We had some sense.

At Inkfluence, the piercing specialist had short, fiery hair and wore a muscle shirt to show off her tattoos. Dragons, flowers, butterflies, serpents wrapped around her shoulders, her collarbone, her biceps, her hands. She made jewelry, she said, and was going to grad school. She knew what she wanted. She was one of the prettiest women I'd ever seen.

I completed the paperwork and signed the waiver. I let her charge $50 to my credit card.

My sister said, "You don't have to do this. No one will think you're chicken. No one will know."

"I'm fine. I want to."

When I was a teenager, my father gave me a pair of diamond earrings so my mother would let me pierce my ears. He drove me to the mall where the saleslady at Rings 'n' Things shot my ears with stud bullets. A flush burnt my face, then traveled to my stomach where it churned into nausea. When she said *pus might seep* from my ears, no, when she said *pus,* period, I collapsed on the floor, a dead faint. Afterward, my father whispered, "Piece of cake. No one will know. Let's don't tell your mother."

And I hadn't told anyone that, lately, I'd been contemplating divorce—or at least fleeing. For weeks, I'd been dismissing my graduate class twenty minutes early every Thursday night. It was a crime my husband would never have suspected because he couldn't imagine me swindling my students, couldn't imagine I would cheat them. While he believed I was lecturing on the history of magazine publication in America, I was really driving my car around the city loop, listening to the radio, and crying. As I'd leave the business lights behind on the east side of town, the night sky opened, and the stars shimmied like drops of water. The highway unfurled before me, white and broad as the belt of the Milky Way. I could have headed up toward Amarillo or kept due north into Oklahoma, Kansas, the Dakotas. I could have crooked west and seen the Pacific Ocean in two days. But my eye stayed focused on the hub of our marriage, and by 9:15 P.M., I always banked the U-turn and went home.

"I'm nearing midlife," I told my sister. "If I can handle a needle stitched through my stomach, I can take control of other things. I'd like to feel stronger. I'd like a symbol."

The piercing specialist marked two dots on my belly, the point of entrance and the exit.

I giggled.

"Ticklish?" she asked.

"Nervous," I said. "I laugh in moments of crisis."

She smiled. "You want a ring or a barbell?"

"I want a gold ring. A perfect circle. One that begins and ends with me."

I climbed on the surgical table. She called it that.

"Lay on your hands," she said. "Put them beneath your back so you're not tempted to slap my arm away during the procedure."

I obeyed but wondered why I was having an operation without anesthesia and a doctor.

She clamped my stomach with forceps. "Whatever you do, don't look at the needle."

I checked my sister who stood beside me, patting my shoulder. Her eyes were round as headlights and pointed in the direction of the needle. "She said not to look at the needle. You're with me. We're both not looking," I told her.

Later, my sister told me she saw the needle all right. But at that moment, my sister, the one who had convinced me BBs wouldn't hurt, strummed her fingers on my shoulder the way she comforted her cat by scratching under its chin. "It's nothing," she assured me. "You can do this." And this time, she meant it.

The specialist pierced my belly, leaning her weight into me, her arm driving the needle as if boring a spike through muscle and bone. The snake tattoo on her left bicep rippled. I could feel my skin stretch at the exit wound, spiking up like a little tent before the needle broke the hide. And I could feel the gauge of the needle. It felt thick as an ice pick.

When I thought she'd finished, she hadn't slipped the ring in yet. She hooked the sliver of gold, sharp as a splinter, through the fresh wound. Tugging at the puncture, she cinched the ring and clamped it shut with a small gold ball. My hands threatened to squirm free, angry and ready to defend my stomach.

"All done." The girl hopped backward. Her hands shot into the air as if she'd roped and tied a calf and knew she'd better jump clear.

My sister offered me a piece of chocolate—a Hershey's Kiss.

"Good plan," the specialist said. "Good idea, that chocolate. You lie there and gobble it up before you go."

We all laughed because the chocolate had melted in my sister's grip and I had to lick it off the foil. When I stood, I looked in the mirror first thing. My shirt was tucked up into my bra, and my pants were undone and folded open like an envelope. The tiny gold ring glistened.

Now I understood why teenagers pierced everything once they got started. When parents and teachers claimed sovereignty over you—every day, every hour, a million rules—it was empowering to punch gold studs in your tongue, your nose, your eyebrows, to staple your body with tags reminding everyone who owned what exactly. My husband might believe a wedding band was a cuff binding my hand to his will, but eventually, fumbling under my shirt, he'd discover this secret ring. When he felt the gold thread of it circling into and out of my flesh, he'd know I was capable of acting on the sly. He'd know I was capable of tolerating the pain of freedom. And he'd be frightened.

That night, when I showered, I locked the bathroom door. Standing in the tub alone, the curtain pulled tight, no worries about intrusion, I stared at the gold ring. Slick from soap, it spun easily in and out of the wound. I hadn't shown my husband yet. I knew that after he stopped grilling me about doing something like that to my body without discussing it first, he would fume. Days later, if I didn't apologize, he'd convince himself the gold ring was a gift for him. Otherwise, how could he manage it? When I cooked dinner, made our bed, vacuumed, paid bills, dressed for work, he would stroll by, tug at my shirt, and growl. In the middle of a movie theater, he'd demand: "Show me." It was a sad thing to be married to a man you didn't want to share your piercing experiences with.

But that night, in the shower, I swore the gold ring was a vow to myself. Soon, maybe not tomorrow, but by summer's end, I'd pack a suitcase and haul it to the car. And when my husband saw me lugging my belongings out of his home, he wouldn't be able to lie to himself any longer. He'd know: a full tank of gas, a fresh oil change; grocery money squandered on a cozy throw or toss pillow, something for another home, but not his, because neither matched anything in the bedroom we shared; a new book, a box of them, all of those pages for a woman to disappear inside; and, months before, a secret trip with a sister who couldn't be trusted, a gold ring pierced into my belly, maybe by a man who lifted my shirt, a man whose hands sealed the deal—these were the first signs that a woman was capable of disobedience.

That was May. In September, my husband stood in the driveway, full of remorse, full of doubt, and stared after my car. My taillights blinked once at the corner. Then I was gone.

There are two ways of meeting difficulties. You alter the difficulties or you alter yourself to meet them.

Phyllis Bottome

Jill Patterson teaches in the Creative Writing Program at Texas Tech University. Her work has recently appeared in Fourth Genre, Colorado Review, South Dakota Review, So to Speak, *and anthologies published by several university presses. She serves as editor of* Iron Horse Literary Review *and as director of the San Juan Writers Workshops in Ouray, Colorado.*

Where did you go that day you left your husband?
When I left my husband in September, I headed to Colorado—a small village, 600 people, in the middle of the San Juan Mountains. It took me several weeks to venture out into public.

At first, I just so enjoyed having a house to myself: no curfew, no diet restrictions, whatever I wanted to watch on TV. Then a girlfriend of mine called and said I had to go back into the world and remember what it was like to have friends in my life who really loved me, who weren't trying to control me. I met a group of horse trainers, and they taught me their cowboy ways and loved me up and made me laugh again. They're still three of my very best friends.

Where are you now in your life?

I'm starting over, learning to handle my solitude and enjoying it, which was something I knew before I married but am having to relearn. I now split my time between Colorado and Texas: the summers in the mountains, the school year in Lubbock where I teach. Someday, I'll move to Colorado permanently. I feel like I leave my better self there every year when I have to return to Texas.

Do you still have the belly-button ring?

Yes. In fact, I just had to have my belly repierced. I had bought a ring with a smaller gauge and didn't realize the hole would grow smaller around it. So when I took the smaller ring out the other day to replace it with a new barbell I had, the barbell wouldn't go in, and the smaller ring wouldn't go back in either. It worked out well because this happened while I was writing this piece—doing it again refreshed my memories for writing the story, and the story gave me the determination to do the piercing again. I don't think I ever want to be without my belly ring. It just means so much to me now.

How to Cry in Italian

❧

Isabel Bearman Bucher

Today, my youngest sat at the piano. She'd been accepted at
the university music school, and now she practiced and lived
there. But she was home today, and she began to play and sing
an Italian aria. I watched from the couch, amazed. "Oh Mio
Caro Babbo." I knew every word, every note. I felt my entire
life and everything that I was coming through in that beautiful,
lyrical voice and in this child with long, black, frizzy hair, who
sang like an angel and pumped the pedals with combat boots.
Deep down, I felt something stir inside me.

• • •

Italians cry. They cry for everything. They laugh when
they cry, and they cry when they laugh. They boo-hoo, roller-
coastering into someone's open arms for the kissy-kissy. They
cry if you go and cry if you come, or even if you don't come or

go. They cry for opera, for music, even if it's Irish and especially if it's about mothers. They cry for *un bel'vino rosso* or a *squisita minestra*—for wine and soup. And they think that anybody who doesn't cry has some basic genetic flaw. The statement, "I'm going to cry," is like some magnificent offering, a wondrous thing. At least, that's the way it was in my family, northern Italians who always insisted they were more reserved. Snotty about everybody who lives south of them, yes. But reserved? I don't think so.

My grandparents arrived by sea from the old country. Nonna cried below for the whole crossing because she was homesick and seasick. Nonno dragged her topside, shoved an American flag in her hand, and pointed to the Statue of Liberty—crying all the while. She promptly threw up over the railing, while my mother and her brother cried because they didn't know why their parents were crying. Nonno patted his chest where he kept the grapevines in wet handkerchiefs, and everybody let 'er rip.

It took them two years of working and saving every penny to get out of New York's Little Italy, where Nonno did common labor and Nonna, a college-educated artist who spoke four languages, worked in shirt factories and taught oil painting and Italian to rich people. The grapevines grew in a pot on the fire escape. They moved north to Branford, Connecticut, to that better life they'd envisioned. Nonno built three houses: one for them, with an art studio for Nonna and spacious attic apartment for Uncle Dee; a house for Mamma when she married; and one for his brother when he came over. And there, the vines took root in the soil.

My brother and I were born into *la famiglia* almost three decades later. It was small-town USA, a meshwork of ethnic smells, rich cultures, strong opinions, prejudices, flag-waving, and tight-lipped, close families, who didn't believe in taking a nickel from anyone or owing it, either. The Italians lived on one side of the street, the Swedes and Norwegians on the other; and a few "Dozayankisses" (those Yankees) were scattered on both sides.

"Doz Norwegian women smoke pipes up there," Nonna whispered out of the side of her mouth, gesturing across the street to the attics. She squinted one eye. "And, they-don't-a-cry."

Neither did the Dozayankisses. They were reserved, quiet. They had Jell-O salads with canned fruit and just a drop of mayo on the very top. They were neat. They didn't have birdbaths or chicken coops, and they didn't blame the gypsies for everything. Their lack of emotion and habit of cutting the crusts off their white, sliced bread made them the object of supper conversation.

"They cut-a-da-best-a-part," stated Nonna with certainty.

"You could make a Michelangelo sculpture out of that white bread," quipped my dad, "and go back ten years later, and it would still be soft."

At this, everybody would laugh until they cried. I cried because I really wanted to eat it. And when I cried, they made judgments because nothing you gave water for was ever right.

"Ooooo! Crocodile tears!" they'd hoot. "Cry for something, not nothing! Come over here! I'll give you something to cry for!"

The crying game approached fever pitch on Saturdays, when the opera was heard live from the New York Met. Everybody gathered around the radio in Nonna's living room with the mandatory paraphernalia: crooked cigars, china cups filled with espresso for the ladies, jelly glasses filled with homemade red wine or the okay thing for women to drink—sweet vermouth aperitif. The house smelled of Romano cheese, Nonna's oil paints, saffron, rosemary, garlic, underarms, and smoke. Any Puccini was a guaranteed squirter. But *La Bohéme?* That was the grand squirt of the world. If Mimi was dying or Pagliacco's heart was breaking, forget it! The whole place broke into woos, wa-was, snorts, sucks, howls, Dios, coughs, blasts, wails, and hiccups.

Somewhere between the Italian soaps and the family Sunday supper, I decided that crying was giving in, weak-minded, too emotional, too—Italian. I hated it when I did it. I wanted to be a skinny, bucked-up, stiff-upper-lipped, pale person, who ate Jell-O instead of endive and dandelion salads. I knew that being small, dark, Italian, and emotional was, well, un-American. First-generation kids are like that. They want to fit in. I made up my mind to stop crying. I obsessed on the phenomenon and studied crying styles like some sort of possessed scientist.

Mamma had a way of biting her finger knuckles, pushing her chin to her chest, and woo-wooing. Nonna copied the Michelangelo paintings of female saints and holy mothers. She was an artist. She placed her right hand over her heart, middle fingers together, and end ones slightly spread. Then the left would go over the right, both wrists arched. She'd crank her head sideways right, rolling suffering eyes up to heaven. "Dio," would be next, then tears. "Aahh-ah-ahya-ya-ya," would wander up and down like an arpeggio scale until she ran out of breath.

My aunt Mimi, married to Crazy Uncle Dee, would make her mouth round and suck in air while tears squirted out. Then something like a high-pitched porpoise whistle would precede hiccups. Prozia Irma, married to Prozio Victor, would puff like a steam engine, and then let 'er go with one big woo-blast.

The men were quieter, at first. But when they cut loose . . . Nonno would grit his perfect thumbnail-sized teeth, like he was going to knock somebody's lights out. Then tears would roll down his rosy cheeks. He'd "Ah-ha-ha-ha-ha," loud out of one side of his mouth, suck up, swallow, and show teeth again, while pushing a wadded hanky to his beak of a nose. His smelly cigar never dropped. Prozio would blow his nose with continuous blasts that would have shattered glass, muffling tsks and bottom teeth whistles, while engaging in abdominal crunches and shoulder hunches. My father's eyes would fill, get red, and he would "Woof-ha, ha, ha, ahahaaaa," cough, cough, cough, then big blow.

The years went by. The grapevines grew wild. The family scattered to the four winds. The old ones passed on, and the rest of us lost contact. I got married, had two girls, became a widow, and remarried. Who I was got buried and forgotten under the years, even when it came into vogue to be "ethnic." I never listened to opera. Crying got a token shot now and again, but it never worked. It all stayed deep inside, like the rest of who I was.

Then, as my children grew, the smells began to bring me back—saffron, olive oil, anise. The involuntary pouring of red wine onto meats and into soups, the preference for grated Romano, the knowing exactly how to use a chef's knife to chop parsley, pound a clove of garlic, and meld them with salt pork for the base of minestrone. I realized that I only wanted to drink red wine and was surprised when my daughters showed the preference, too. We took to very strong *caffè robusto*. I found myself listening to the opera on Saturday errands in the car. Out of my mouth came fragments of songs in Italian.

Then came that day—the day my daughter sat down at the piano to play.

I bit my knuckle. I sucked in air. My eyes filled to overflowing. I clasped my hands over my heart and whispered, "Dio." I put my hands over my mouth to try to keep it in. I did abdominal crunches and shoulder hunches, squeaked a porpoise whistle, then woo-blasted so loud, I was gasping for air. I wandered up the scale, while the tears squirted out, splashed all over my lap and onto the table. I blew my beak of a nose. Hiccups followed, naturally. And that day, I let 'er rip for thirty-five years, for Nonno, for Nonna, for Mamma and Dad. I said "phooey" for Uncle Dee and cried a bit more for Mimi, Prozia Irma, and Prozio Vic. *God, how I missed them.* And my singing daughter? She never missed a note, carrying on with her practice as if her crying mother were the most natural thing in the world.

I cry for everything now, not for nothing, because I have everything. I cry when my daughters say I was a good mamma, for a beautiful soup, sunsets and sunrises, for flowing and dulcet arias, for humanity. I fly into the arms of my longtime friends for the kissy-kissy and tear up watching my healthy husband snore softly on the couch even before the ten o'clock news. And the crying winds back through the corridors of time, whispering through the generations—all of us—whose hearts are full to breaking because of pride and beauty and feeling. And now I know why Italians cry.

Family faces are magic mirrors. Looking at people who belong to us, we see the past, present, and future.

Gail Lumet Buckley

Isabel Bearman Bucher lives with her husband in Albuquerque, New Mexico. When she is not doing aerobics or backpacking with her longtime girlfriends, she loves cooking and just being. Isabel recently completed Nonno's Monkey, *a memoir of her life as a small child in an Italian-American family. She is writing her first work of fiction,* Tafoya's Laundromat, *set in Taos.*

Where do you live now, and what brought you there?
When I was still quite young, we left *la famiglia* and moved to boomtown Houston, Texas. My dad felt he'd never seen the world and wanted to go somewhere to "be somebody." That always confused me as a child because he already was a huge somebody in my life. Our life was then a lonely one, fraught with a kind of prejudice we'd never known and couldn't understand. To that world, we were "funny-talking dark people" who ate strange things and had uppity ideas. The loss of the close extended family was a grief that lay buried for years in our family. Then, when I was seventeen, we moved to New Mexico, where life improved for us all.

Have you been back to visit the old family property in Connecticut?

I went back with my husband and friends last fall. The three homes Nonno built are still there. The people whom Nonno sold to all those years ago still live there.

Whatever happened to the grapevines?

They're still on the property, gone wild. I've asked my cousin to obtain a cutting of the vines, and I expect an overnight package soon. My daughter, the singer, plans to become a sommelier. She tells me that the grape is called Nebbiolo, one of the oldest varieties historically known on earth, guarded fiercely and not allowed out of Italy anymore. Like Nonno, I am a gardener and hear him whispering right behind me as I tend things.

Please share with us your favorite Italian supper.

For most Italians, food, family, and music are everything. To the women in my family, the Sunday supper was a sacred offering to those whom they loved most in all the world—and also to those guests just off the boat from Italy or from the local Italian community. Northern Italians are primarily vegetarians. So on Sundays, we ate risotto, rice with saffron, mushrooms, white wine, chicken broth, and fresh-grated Reggiano Parmesan. Then came the veal, pounded thin, insalata mista—very bitter greens, endive, maybe arugula or spring dandelions dressed with balsamic and green, green olive oil. Black ground pepper was a must. Nonno's wine poured freely. I still make that supper for the people whom I love the most, and when I do, I know Mamma, Mimi, Nonna, and Prozia Irma are smiling.

Take This Job

⚘

Emma Troy

I was not supposed to need a job. As the happily married mother
of two, my destiny was to drive my small Beamer SUV around
the suburbs, from my big house with the pool in the back to
my kids' private school to Starbucks and Nordstrom's and back
again, in my designer yoga togs. All day, every day.

And then, the clock struck midnight, and *poof* my Cinder-
ella life was over. So much for destiny. No husband, no money,
no future—but two kids to support on my so-called skill as a
freelance writer. Which meant I had a couple of old newspaper
clippings of articles I'd written before my doomed marriage and
a slew of deservedly unpublished short stories on my laptop.
Not exactly an impressive portfolio. I hadn't had a real job since
right after college—and that was in banking, a field in which I
had little interest or aptitude.

We needed to eat. But the job market was tough, even for
far more experienced people than I. So I rewrote my resume,

making as much an art of euphemism as I dared. I sold the boat, and sent the resume out to every company in California, and waited. *Nada.* I sold the big-screen TV, and sent my resume out to every company in the West, and waited. *Zip.* I sold the piano, and sent my resume out to every company in the free world, and waited. *Nothing.*

I was running out of time—and I was already out of luck. The State of California prevented my moving back home to Indiana with my kids, even though my husband had disappeared off the face of the planet. My lawyer advised patience and petitioned the court again, but then the poor man dropped dead before the hearing. (You know what they say, "The only thing worse than a bad lawyer is a dead one.") The creditors were closing in on me, and I had already sold most of everything we owned.

The day I put the "for sale" sign on the swing set, I decided that desperate measures were in order.

Time to redo my cover letter! I had tried every kind of cover letter in the *Cover Letters That Knock 'Em Dead* handbook my attorney had given me before his untimely demise—to no avail. Enough euphemism! What this situation called for was a little creative writing. To wit: I decided to tell the truth.

Dear Hiring Manager,

It's been kind of a rough year for me so far. My car was repossessed, my house went into foreclosure, and my husband left me for a guy named Jim. And it's only February.

In other words, I need a job.

*I have two small children to support on my own. But don't
let that stop you. I'm strong as a horse, smart as a whip,
and motivated as hell. Give me a job, and I'll work like a
dog for you.*

*Enclosed please find a copy of my resume and some sample
clips. If you have any questions, do feel free to contact me
at any time. I look forward to hearing from you.*

Sincerely,
Emma Troy

I sent new packets out with the revised cover letter to more
than 100 publications in northern California. Two weeks later,
I got a call from a Mr. Tom Owens, Executive Editor of *Small
Business,* a magazine out of San Luis Obispo.

"You don't have any real experience," he told me. "But you
can write. I'll give you a week's trial. You'll get a letter in the
mail confirming it later this week."

Thank you! I arranged for my mom to fly out from Indiana to
watch the kids and packed my bags. Long before dawn, I donned
my best suit and started out across the Santa Cruz Mountains and
down the Pacific Coast Highway to San Luis Obispo, thanking
Jesus, Moses, Buddha, Allah, and Mother Teresa for this wonderful opportunity to make $18,000 a year as an editorial assistant.

My cell phone rang at 7:00 A.M., just as I was approaching the
city limits. I pulled over to the side of the road. It was Mr. Owens.

"I'm sorry, Ms. Troy, but the week's trial offer is off. Don't
bother coming in."

"But why?" I was practically in tears.

"In the editorial department, we all loved your cover letter. We thought it was funny and creative," he said. "But our CEO saw it and flipped out. He said it was unprofessional, and he didn't want anyone who'd write that sort of letter working for his organization."

"Oh." I switched the phone off and got out of the car, tearing through the brush to the beach. I sank down into the sand and cried. I cried for about thirty minutes. Then I stopped. Crying was getting me nowhere. I'd been looking for a job for months, and this was my first bite. I couldn't afford to let it go.

If I'd learned anything from my poor lawyer before he died, it was *get it in writing*. And I had it in writing, a letter from Mr. Owens confirming my week's trial. They'd honor my week's trial—or I'd sue their asses with my dead lawyer's junior partner. I brushed the tears from my cheeks and the sand from my skirt and got back in the car. San Luis Obispo had not heard the last of me.

A week later, I had a job. My threat to sue them should they not honor my week's trial worked like a charm. And I worked like a dog that week, just as I'd promised in my cover letter, and by the end of those five sixteen-hour workdays, the CEO himself dropped by my desk to shake my hand.

"I hear that you're one heck of a good writer," he told me, his Trump-esque silver bouffant gleaming over me.

"Thank you. It's a great publication." I smiled sweetly at him and willed him to hire me.

Which he did. I stayed there at the business magazine two years, during which time Mr. Owens taught me everything I know about writing and editing. When I was ready to move on to bigger and more lucrative opportunities, he took me to lunch to celebrate on my last day there.

"May I ask you a personal question?" he said over dessert and coffee.

"Sure."

"Was any of it true?" Mr. Owens looked at me, a mix of sheepishness and concern on his face.

"You mean in the cover letter?"

"Yeah."

"Off the record?"

Mr. Owens grinned at me. "Off the record."

I grinned back. "Every word."

"Unbelievable."

I leaned forward. "I want to thank you for taking a chance on me. I really needed the job."

Tom chuckled. "When you showed up to fight for it, I knew I had to hire you—whether you could write or not. Lucky for me you could."

"No, Tom, lucky for me."

You make your own luck—another thing my dead lawyer used to say. I like to think that wherever he is now, up in that great courtroom in the sky, he's looking down on me and smiling. I did him proud, may he rest in peace.

‰

Nothing risqué, nothing gained.

Jayne Mansfield

Emma Troy is a writer, editor, and novelist whose work has taken her from the West Coast to the East Coast and back again. The author of two books and midwife to hundreds more, she now works in Boston, where she acquires and develops book projects for a major publisher. Happily single, she lives in the country with her children, two dogs, and a cat, where she's hard at work on a memoir of her love-cursed life.

You've come a long way since fighting for your first job. Does that experience continue to inform your work?

Occasionally. I'm not a fighter by nature; I still tend to avoid conflict whenever possible, preferring the arts of negotiation and persuasion to confrontation. But I have learned that there are times when my only recourse is to fight—and fight to win. Motherhood has emboldened me; I find myself waging battles on my kids' behalf that I would never have waged for myself alone. I needed to feed my children—that's what propelled me into the *Small Business* offices to demand my week's trial. Without the kids as impetus, I may have just gone back home to bed and cried for a week. But I didn't—and by standing up for them, I learned to stand up for myself, as well.

Would you advise other job seekers to be so brutally honest about their circumstances in their cover letters?

I was honest, but more important, I was funny. I made Tom Owens laugh, and that's what got me the week's trial. Humor is a formidable weapon; what you can't get with honey, you can often get with humor. That said, desperate times do call for desperate measures—and I was desperate. My choice was this: Get a job or go on welfare. My cover letter was, admittedly, wild. But it worked. It highlighted my ability to write, revealing an immature talent that Tom knew could develop into something more—with his help. That's what a cover letter should do.

Are you still in contact with Tom?
I ran into him at an airport not long ago. He told me that *Small Business* had been sold to some outfit in the Midwest. He's still in California, doing very well in corporate writing.

Meanwhile, your career has taken off. Are you surprised by your success?
I am surprised—and grateful—that I've been able to make a decent living doing something I truly love. I was very content as a housewife; I loved being home with my kids. I went back to work only as a last resort, believing that eventually I'd remarry and be a stay-at-home mom again. That never happened. Which is just as well, because I fell in love with the publishing world, and thus became ambitious in my own right.

Since your husband left you, have you found love?
I have found love from time to time, but not the lasting kind that lends itself to marriage. At least not yet. I remain hopeful—if not altogether optimistic—that someday I'll find a man with whom I can share my life and my kids. As it turns out, it's a lot easier for me to get a good job than it is for me to find a good man. Go figure.

8,000 Miles Off the Map

❧

Jessica Hayden

"I'll marry Tom Cruise," I decided, "even though I know he was your husband last time."

"I can't believe you're stealing Tom," Katie pouted, a look she'd already perfected by the age of twelve.

The three of us sat on the floor of my friend Beth's bedroom. Stuck inside on a rainy day, we had pulled out scratch paper to play MASH—Mansion, Apartment, Shack, or House—mapping out our entire lives, starting with our future homes. From there, it went on to husband (usually a choice between the cute high school quarterback, the hottest TV actors, and maybe someone you actually had a crush on), car, and number of offspring. By the end, through a scientific process of elimination, you'd have the perfect outline of your life.

Of course, the game was absurd, and you'd often end up marrying an NFL quarterback but living in a shack in Montana with fourteen kids. And how you planned to pay for that Ferrari and yearly vacation to the Cayman Islands was anyone's guess.

Fortunately, the results of our dream planning never had any real impact on our lives. Yet somehow, the concept of taking pen and paper and mapping out the "who, what, when, where, and why" of our futures seemed to take root at an early age.

While I never wrote it down, I certainly had a rock-solid map for my future by the time I reached high school. I would graduate at the top of my class, win a field hockey scholarship to an academically prestigious school, meet the perfect man my sophomore year, spend a year or two working, go to law school, marry my college sweetheart, and start having kids around twenty-eight, while still on the partner track at my first-rate law firm. And maybe I'd run for Congress someday. It was all so simple.

Or was it?

It was the day before Christmas when I got the call. "Jess, your *boyfriend* is on the phone," my sister screeched, with a leering emphasis on the word "boyfriend." In our mid-twenties, we were both way past the age where having a boyfriend should be fodder for jokes, but we still acted like we were in the fifth grade.

Giddily, I picked up the kitchen phone, the same one we had since I was in kindergarten with the rotary dial and the long, spiral cord. I walked into our living room, nervously twirling the cord around my fingers.

Liam and I had been dating for about six months. We had met my second year out of college in Washington, D.C., where I was working on political campaigns. I'd joined a kickball league on a whim, and after our first game, we met at the league happy hour. He was everything I was looking for: cute, funny, wickedly smart, athletic, and adventurous.

For a month, I would hold my breath waiting for those Wednesday evenings when I knew I'd see him again. He'd buy me a drink after the game. We'd flirt. I had butterflies every time I'd catch his glance. Within no time at all, we were in love. Big time.

There was just one problem. I had been accepted to law school, chugging away according to that life map, and he had just joined the Foreign Service and could soon be posted somewhere far, far away. He expected to get his assignment sometime around Christmas, and although he had asked for my input on where I'd be willing to live (Monaco: yes; Saudi Arabia: no) I was still unsure whether or how far I was willing to travel for love. While I kept my fingers crossed for Canada, I knew I was making empty wishes.

"So I found out today," he excitedly reported.

I held my breath.

"They are sending me to Kazakhstan!"

"Congratulations," I exclaimed. I wanted to say more, but I realized that I had no earthly idea where the hell Kazakhstan was. Put a map in front of me and I'd have probably looked in South America.

I hung up the phone and went online to *Google* this previously unknown "stan." There it was, a country as large as Western Europe, sitting between Russia and China. I noticed Afghanistan hanging out a bit to the south and Pakistan and India nearby. *Great neighborhood,* I thought.

But my concern went beyond geopolitics. Even though we had only been dating for six months, I was pretty sure this was the guy. But there was also my career, law school, my plans for the corner office. Was I ready to give it all up for a country I could barely pronounce?

For the next few months, I was a walking conflict. Excited about law school, thrilled about Liam, crushed about the Foreign Service, confused about my path. One day, I'd wander into the travel section of Barnes & Noble and read everything I could find on Kazakhstan. The next, I'd be researching law firms, planning my post-law-school life. I wanted both my dream career and my dream husband. I wasn't ready to give up either of them.

On a particularly beautiful spring afternoon, I took a break from work and walked down to the corner coffee shop. I ordered a snack and sat at one of the sidewalk tables, watching the world go by. I thought back to those lazy afternoons playing MASH in my best friend's bedroom, and realized that even though we were playing a child's game, the ethos it espoused had drastically affected my life. I had devised a plan and was psychologically wed to it.

Moving to Kazakhstan was never on my list of goals. In fact, it was never even a blip on my radar screen. But then again, why did everything have to comport with some prototype of my perfect life? Maybe it was time to get rid of that pesky map and go where the road took me. I might risk getting a little lost from time to time, but my bet was, in the long run, I'd find my way.

That night, instead of worrying about my decision, I took out a piece of paper, a few fashion magazines, and scissors.

I was making a homemade greeting card, and I flipped through the pages to find the right letters. When I was done, I looked proudly at my "masterpiece."

When I met Liam for dinner the next night, I presented my gift with a flourish.

He looked at me slyly. "What's this for? It's not my birthday. It's not Valentine's Day—or is it and I've just totally screwed up?"

"Nope!" I replied, happy to keep him guessing.

He ripped open the envelope and pulled out my multi-colored creation. The front read, "Congratulations!" The inside:

The bearer of this card is entitled to one weekend retreat to the famous Lake Balkhash, located in little known but fabulously romantic Kazakhstan.

He looked up and smiled crookedly. "So, Lake Balkhash, huh? How did you hear about it?"

"Well, I looked on a map, and it was the only lake I could find. I figured they must have some nice weekend retreat spots. We could get massages, go for long hikes. What do you think?"

"What do I think?" His pause seemed like a lifetime. "I think that we'll have to stay out of the water because I'm pretty sure that, during the Soviet rule, they had some sort of nuclear disaster near there.

And with that, I threw out my map—and stopped relying on them to pick vacation spots.

A year later, we boarded a Boeing 747 out of Dulles, Virginia, headed for Kazakhstan, and we've been here ever since.

Georgetown granted me a leave of absence, and this fall, I'll return to finish my degree and Liam will serve a tour at the State Department in Washington. After that, who knows? We're still figuring it all out. It won't be easy managing two careers, a family, and a life of moving from country to country. But is it easy for anyone? I often think back to the day when I chose to follow my heart instead of my map—and how it has opened up a world of joy and fulfillment I never knew existed.

I've certainly learned that road maps can be useful when trying to get your bearings on foreign backcountry roads, but they are less so when trying to get your bearings in life. So what if life takes you far off the road you thought you'd travel? The roads can be a little bumpier over here, but I have a secret—the air is cleaner, the vistas more stunning, and life is simply more beautiful.

The strongest principle of growth
lies in the human choice.

George Eliot

After spending two years in Kazakhstan, Jessica Hayden now lives in Washington, D.C. While she misses the opportunity to eat kazy *and* kumus *(horse sausage and camel's milk), she enjoys sushi in a city that's closer to the ocean. While in Kazakhstan,*

Jessica worked for the United States Agency for International Development (USAID), where she traveled to some of the most remote regions of Central Asia, including Kyrgyzstan and the Silk Road cities of Bukhara and Samarkand in Uzbekistan. Jessica writes about legal issues, foreign affairs, and travel. After law school, Jessica hopes to head overseas again with her husband Liam, although she's doing her best not to map out any plans.

Share some of your adventures in Kazakhstan.

In my two years there, I survived having my appendix removed in a tent, an SUV-horse collision, trekking in some of the most remote mountains in Central Asia, traveling to the Afghan-Uzbek border for my work with USAID, and, of course, my first two years of marriage.

How did living abroad affect your marriage?

One of the most drastic things about moving so far away right after Liam and I were married was the immediate change in our social support system. In Washington, I had my own family and my own friends. For the first few months, as we figured things out together, we really had to rely on each other to get through the hard times—and learn how to communicate. I would say overall, it was a great way to start our marriage and helped us form a really solid foundation.

What were some of the worst things about living in Central Asia?

Although we were incredibly lucky to have so many of our friends and family make the twenty-four-hour flight out there, it was sometimes hard to be so far from the States, especially on holidays or when a big event happened back home that we just couldn't attend. I missed so many births and weddings. But, on the other hand, it made reunions that much more special.

What were some of the best things?
Almaty is nestled into 14,000-foot mountains, and often, as I drove to work, I couldn't imagine a more beautiful place. As a former outdoor enthusiast, I reconnected with nature and took up camping and trekking again. In addition to the natural beauty, living in Central Asia exposed me to a culture that I would never have learned about otherwise.

So, did living in such a different culture change your outlook on life?
I think I've become a much stronger person by being there and developed a thicker skin. There were so many experiences that pushed me outside of my comfort zone and made me reevaluate what I think and why I think it. For example, I traveled in Kyrgyzstan to Osh and Jalalabad, part of a region known for more radical elements of Islam, where political tensions flared in the early nineties and several people were killed in riots. Before I started this trip, I was worried about my safety. But soon after landing and meeting with local villagers, I felt so welcomed into their homes that it really changed my perspective on what this part of the world is like. Instead of hostility, I found an openness and kindness that was almost overwhelming.

Out West, Ain't It?

Ellen Waterston

Because I said I would, I would dedicate myself to the man on whom I had pinned my fantasy of ranch life, a fantasy that was eroding faster than the sandy banks could collapse into the Musselshell during spring run off. (I let the storm door slam behind me as I struggled out with a pail of garbage for the pigs.) Because I said I would, I would dedicate myself to that cock-eyed blue heeler, lying, legs splayed; the yard light that twitched on and off at twilight; the shed full of nervous chickens, feathers blown inside out by the wind coming off the Missouri breaks.

Because never in my twenty-six years had I been married, castrated a bull calf, herded cows, or lived eighty miles from groceries, I had to rely on my husband's take on things. "This is out West, ain't it?" he said, leaning forward over the steering wheel and sending a straight stream of brown tobacco spit into a tin can on the floorboard. I heard it as a statement, not a question.

I would, I vowed, cook better, ride harder, be tougher, even fuck where making love had been what I dreamed would untuck the sheets. I had thought all would turn out as beautifully as the stars that yawned across the Montana sky at night, as romantically as that summer on the dude ranch where I first met Rob. "Make a hand!" he barked as I tried unsuccessfully to coax the mare out of the trailer.

Charlie Hall arrived early. I had figured out ranchers did this to catch their neighbor on the "bed ground." To avoid this possibility, Rob, pulling on his jeans, would stagger outside before dawn and light the burn barrel or create some other sign of life and then climb back into bed half-dressed. Rob heard the truck pull up, was at the door in a shot.

"Cold in earnest, wouldn't you say?"

"I would," responded Charlie, deadpan, walking in.

"Meet my bride," Rob said.

"Heard," stated Charlie. "Be damned," he concluded, running his eyes over me as I hastily tied my bathrobe.

"Where's Delores?" Rob asked.

Charlie shifted a toothpick to the other side of his mouth and pointed toward the door with his lips.

"She'll freeze!" I interjected.

Charlie didn't respond.

"Ellie, coffee," Rob demanded.

I poured them both a cup and slipped on my coat. The windows of Charlie's pickup were steamed. I awkwardly knocked on the driver's side. In small, jerky increments, the window rolled down to reveal Delores, her hairdo secured by a turquoise chiffon scarf. She sat, one blue-jeaned leg on either side of the stick shift, looking straight ahead through a faded black garter suspended from the rearview mirror.

"Would you like to come inside?"

Delores looked at me and then back at the flat horizon. "Pleased to meet you."

"Oh, sorry, I'm Ellie." I added: "I made a pot of coffee."

"In?" questioned Delores. "Heavens no, men got their business. Knowin' them, they'll have a cuppa two 'fore they get down to it. Likely I'll be froze by then." There was a long pause. "What do you make of this country?" asked Delores as though noticing it for the first time. "Up here *Northside* plenty desolate, ain't it." I looked around my new home with the desolation in mind—the hieroglyph of corrals tattooed on the treeless scape, the sullen windmill, the dilapidated chicken coop perched on blocks of cement.

"Why, where do you live?" I asked Delores.

Delores puffed up, the zipper of her purple windbreaker straining across her bosom. "South of the river. Lordy. *Southside.*"

"Near Custer?" I still wasn't sure of my bearings.

Delores wouldn't deign an answer. "Can't imagine the grass very strong here. And not a tree! Tough on calvin'." Delores shook her head.

Rob and Charlie interrupted our chilly sentinel.

"Finally," grumbled Delores. And then, addressing the dashboard, "Custer Handicrafters are looking for you to join up. First Tuesday every month."

I realized Charlie was standing behind me, waiting to get in his truck. I eased toward the back of the pickup and, to mask my embarrassment, reached to pat his Border collie. Charlie growled, "Ain't Rob instructed you? Don't be pettin' another man's stock dog." He looked at Rob and cocked his head toward the collie. "Bitch is bred."

Rob put his arm around me. "Not a bad idea." I pulled away.

Charlie and Delores drove off, their truck soon vanishing off the edge of the landscape. Rob pressed a kiss on my cold lips. "Don't be losing your sense of humor, now."

I thought seriously about losing it the morning of the Custer Handicrafters meeting. Rob's only advice was to remember not to pet Charlie's dog, a story that was wearing thin. "And I should tell you," he added, "better yell or honk before you set foot on their property. Been known to shoot before they look." I believed it of Delores but was determined to go. I wanted to meet the women of this far-flung community of ranches and to establish myself among them, individually, separate from Rob.

I drove the forty miles of dirt road, crossing to the south side of the Yellowstone River and, just shy of Custer, turned into the Hall's driveway. I pulled up in front of the blindingly white and meticulously kept ranch house, dwarfed by an array of outbuildings.

"Hello! Anyone home?" I abruptly pulled my head back inside the pickup and slouched down in case anyone really was armed and dangerous. Nothing happened. I consulted my watch. I was a bit early. After a few moments, I repeated the performance, this time honking twice.

Delores filled the entire door frame with her incredulity. "What the hell you want, escorted?"

"Oh my God," I muttered under my breath. "I'll kill him."

"Well, come in then," Delores gestured impatiently.

I followed Delores into the living room, which featured a small side table displaying a vase full of peacock feathers next to a beige La-Z-Boy recliner. On a coffee table in front of an olive green sofa was a bud vase holding a small American flag.

The other women had begun to arrive. Twila, a large, plain woman dressed in a worn cotton shirt with a faded floral pattern on it, was the only one who introduced herself to me.

"Say, you must be Rob's wife, up there Northside." I looked into a ferocious-looking face—like the Duchess in *Alice in Wonderland.* "Only two of us here, Northsiders, that is. We'd better stick together." Twila eased herself into a chair dwarfed by her big frame. "Never know why I come. Never have any luck at them craft projects they do. Like to socialize ever so often, though." I nodded in agreement. Twila was gaining steam. "Knowin' Rob, he'd surely pick a savvy gal who'd be out and about. You're probably like me, rather be out and about than in here, right?"

"I'm not sure how impressed Rob is with my out and about."

"Oh, fiddlesticks. Question is, are you?" Twila paused, studied me more closely. "You new to this way of life, right?"

I nodded.

"From the East, I hear?"

I nodded again.

"Must be something you always dreamed of doing, to come as far from your kind as you did." Twila settled further back in her chair. "That's wonderful," she said dreamily. "Knowin' what you want, committing yourself to it."

Words to live by. It hit me that I hadn't. But I would—starting right then. The realization provoked a sudden wave of emotion. I hoped Twila wouldn't notice, but she did.

"My, my," said Twila in such a sensitive tone it was all I could do not to succumb to tears. "Course . . . and . . ." Twila bought some time, hunting the ceiling for something to say. She found it. "Now I'll tell you *what.* I've had it with this Northside, Southside nonsense. Holdover from the Dust Bowl days is what it is, when no one wanted the land we're makin' a fine living on now, a *fine* livin'." She peered at me. I smiled to signal I was going to be all right.

From the other end of the table, Delores called the meeting to order.

Twila continued in a loud whisper. "Think people get past that sort of thing, now wouldn't you? Well, they don't. Don't know how it is in your New York City. But here? Some just need to feel higher up."

Delores gave Twila a silencing look. In unison, all the women stood and placed their hands over their hearts and recited the Pledge of Allegiance, their eyes trained on the small flag. Next, the Lord's Prayer, each woman looking earnestly at the carpet.

"Any old business?" Delores inquired. The room remained silent. "New? None? Well, I have some. Our guest and hopefully newest Handicrafter, Ellie!" She gestured toward me.

The seven women applauded politely, like rain into a pie tin. I half stood and then sat. "Thank you . . . and I look forward to becoming a . . . Handicrafter?"

"Well then," Delores said. "Let's show Ellie what being a Handicrafter is all about!"

The women relocated around the table, squealing in appreciation of the tiny mouse displayed in the center made of two small marbles, bits of thread for whiskers, a piece of felt for the tail, and tiny beads for the eyes. Delores presided. "Seeing as it will soon be that time of year when the field mice will be thick, I thought it would be fun to make a scare mouse!" The women laughed. "Each of you will need one large marble for the body and one small one for the head." As she spoke, she darted around the table, squirting dollops of glue on a small square of paper at each place. Soon the women quieted in deference to their task.

As I tried to coax the eye bead into position, I noticed Twila was becoming very agitated. Her chair creaked with increasing regularity as she shifted her considerable weight back and forth. Finally, she let her hands drop down on the table in total exasperation; speckles, marbles, thread, and beads stuck to each finger. "I'd rather be sloppin' hogs!" she cried out. "I can't work them tiny marbles with hands such as these," and she extended her weathered, puffy hands as evidence. "Sure like to," she admitted, calmer now. "But those tiny, tiny . . ." Twila bunched her thick fingers together and searched for words to express just how small. Finding none, she just shook her head.

Delores announced that refreshments were ready. All left the table except Twila and me.

"Sorry about that," Twila apologized.

"That's okay," I said.

We shared a laugh about her predicament. I knew I had found a friend, one who had sailed these prairie seas, knew the prevailing winds. She had the air and familiarity of someone I had known a long time, who welcomed me for who I was. This mattered as I struggled to remember that very thing in the newness of life with Rob.

Twila thought for a minute. "I mean, I'm not against trying new things, getting out of my comfort area, like they say. But it's probably not a good idea to get this far out. Never a good idea to get *too* far out of your territory, like I am here. Things get jangled. Have to begin all over. Nothin' what used to works anymore." She looked at me. "You liking this?"

I shrugged.

"Yeah. Probably too soon for you to know." Twila continued. "I always think, this time it will be different at club. Never is. My hands don't get no smaller. Can't force a fit. Things aren't meant to keep goin' wrong for very long. If they do, it's time to move on." She heaved herself up and out of the chair.

After a cup of punch and some cookies and pie, I thanked Delores and got back into the pickup and drove the dirt miles home. Some of what Twila said that day and over the course of our friendship would float to the top of my thoughts on mornings when I cast cornmeal to the chickens across the frozen ground. Some of what Twila said would return me to myself. Some of what Twila said would save me.

I suppose the pleasure of country life lies really in the eternally renewed evidences of the determination to live.

Vita Sackville-West

As a New Englander who married and moved to the ranching West, Ellen Waterston's writing is rooted in both of those cultural and geographic landscapes. Her poems, short stories, and essays have appeared in numerous reviews and anthologies. A chapbook of Waterston's poetry, I Am Madagascar, *was published in 2004 by Ice River Press. Her memoir,* Then There Was No Mountain: The Parallel Odyssey of a Mother and Daughter Through Addiction *(Rowman and Littlefield, 2003), was named one of the top ten books of 2003 in the Northwest by the* Oregonian *and earned her an interview with Diane Sawyer on* Good Morning America *in January 2004.*

How did Twila's words save you?
You know the saying: "When the student is ready, the teacher appears." Twila was like that for me. Although much of what she said didn't sink in until later—so maybe the student wasn't completely ready! But she headed me in the right direction in terms of the importance of getting to know oneself, that things shouldn't go wrong for too long.

How long did that marriage and life last?
The marriage lasted seventeen years (slow learner). When it ended, so did my life as a ranch woman.

What has happened in your life since then?
I raised and supported three children. I now increasingly dedicate my time to my own writing. I had a memoir and a collection

of poetry published within the last two years and am currently working on a novel. I recently started an enterprise called The Writing Ranch, which offers retreats and seminars to support emerging writers.

What was the toughest thing about life on the prairie?
In retrospect, the toughest thing was the isolation. In adverse circumstances, isolation can contribute to distorted thinking. Also, accepting the violence of nature—coyotes killing new-born calves, horses cut on barbed wire, deadly blizzards—that sort of thing.

Your fondest memory?
Oddly, it is the reverse of the toughest things. I came to deeply love the land of the ranching West and now intentionally create opportunities to hole up in the spaciousness and isolation. I have a different relationship with both now. I also came to find real beauty in the rigor of nature, in the no-nonsense of it, in the checks and balances—even in the face of mankind's interference, it constantly tries to right itself.

The Big Question

❧

Kathy Briccetti

In the back seat next to me, Benjamin and his preschool buddy, James, are singing rhymes about dinosaurs pooping as we barrel across the San Francisco Bay Bridge into a thick shroud of summer fog. Our mission: the new dinosaur exhibit at the museum in Golden Gate Park. In his car seat up front with my partner, our one-year-old makes motor razzing sounds at each truck and motorcycle we pass.

We emerge from the Treasure Island tunnel, and a lull in the chatter of the three-year-olds lends a moment of calm. The fog is floating back toward the ocean for its daily intermission, and the spear point of the Transamerica pyramid has jabbed clear through into the blue. If the fog retreats far enough, we might picnic at the children's playground after the exhibit. Just as I begin to drift into my own thoughts, James, a boy from a traditional mom and dad family, breaks the silence.

"So Benjamin, do you have a dad?"

Pam and I lock eyes in the rearview mirror. She raises her eyebrows, and I widen my eyes to say, *Oh boy, here it is. This is big. This is important. What do we do now?* We've talked about what to say at this moment, but it's all left me now. I'm excited, but uneasy. I want to do this right.

None of Benjamin's friends have asked about our family yet. They know I'm Benjamin's "mommy" and Pam is his "mama," and so far, if Benjamin gets any reaction from his pals, it resembles envy. Two mothers. To a preschooler, it doesn't get much better than that. But, now, will James say something that will hurt Benjamin's feelings?

I glance at my son. I want to jump in and answer for him, take care of this, make sure he feels all right about it. But instead, I take a deliberate breath and wait.

"No, I have two women." His voice is buoyant and unencumbered.

"Oh," James says. "But you have to have a dad."

"No. I have two moms." Benjamin sounds less sure now, as if there's suddenly something wrong. I ache for him but don't know whether to interfere. Plus I'm curious about what he'll say, how he understands all of this.

James is silent for a minute, but he's not finished. His little forehead is scrunched up with three-year-old thinking. "Did your dad die, Benjamin?"

"No."

Silence. "Yeah, he must have died, cuz you don't have one."

Benjamin looks up at me. His expression says, *What do I say here?*

I can't wait any longer. "Do you want me to help explain it to James?"

His features relax. "Yes."

"James, do you know how you have a sister and Benjamin has a brother?"

"Yeah."

"You know how some families have cats and some have dogs?"

"My cat's name is Bella."

Benjamin jumps in. "Our dog is Chesie!"

In the front seat, the baby echoes, "Sessie!"

"Well, some families have a mom and a dad, some have two moms or two dads, and some might have just a mom or a dad." I don't go into all the possible configurations. Grandparents. Foster families. The sperm bank and adoption stories can wait for later. Will it be all right with his parents that I'm telling him this?

In the late nineties, we're trailblazers in the "Gayby Boom," not at the front of the pack, but near it. We have few role models and no books telling us how to do this. We know other two-mom families, but strangely, we're the only one in Benjamin's Berkeley preschool class. I want to keep this conversation light, not project my fears onto my children. *Don't make them feel ashamed. Keep it simple. No big deal.*

But it is a big deal, a huge deal.

When Pam and I talked about having children, I worried that having two moms would mess them up, scar them for life. My mother had told me about the only lesbian couple in Indianapolis she knew. "Their son is a little strange," she said with a grimace. "I think he may have psychological problems."

"Well, maybe there are other reasons for that," I said. I fought the hot anger building in my face. "Children of straight couples have psychological problems, too." Although I was nervous about what we were planning to do—inseminating with the help of a sperm bank and raising children without a father—I couldn't admit this to her. "Maybe he's having problems because of people's reaction to his family. Homophobia." I announced this with the confidence of an expert on a panel. I had to project an assured air, no matter that it scared me sometimes, what we were doing. I had to defend my decision to bring up a child in a different kind of family, one that wasn't recognized by many and was disdained by others.

I once debated with another lesbian couple about whether we're making our kids suffer because we've made them fatherless. They said yes, definitely. I disagreed. How can you grieve over something you never lost? But I also know I'm too close to it. Just because our kids don't tell us it bothers them doesn't mean that's the case.

What would James say next? Have I told him what he wanted to know, or is he not buying it? Have I said enough? Too much?

"Oh," James whispers. Deep in thought, he gazes out the window at the San Francisco skyline. We're closing in on the exit to the park. "I hope I get to see a brontosaurus," he says. "That's my favorite. The brontosaurus."

❧

Are anybody's parents typical?

Madeleine L'Engle

Kathy Briccetti is a freelance writer living in the San Francisco Bay area. Her essays, book reviews, and opinion pieces have appeared in local, national, and online publications, as well as on public radio. She is at work on a memoir about three generations of fatherless children and adoption in her family. She is a student in the Stonecoast MFA program in creative writing.

Has Benjamin faced "The Big Question" often since then?

Ben just turned twelve. Last fall, he left his cozy, K-5 elementary school with around 300 students for a middle school of 900. Every time we leave one school for the next, we're thrust into the larger world, and our community gets bigger. First, it was moving from preschool to what seemed, at the time, a huge elementary school. But despite my fretting, his having two moms and no dad was never an issue there. By the time he reached fifth grade at the elementary school, there were a dozen or so gay-parented families and, of course, many adopted children, several children with single parents, and some being raised by grandparents. I feel lucky to live in a community that is so diverse, both ethnically and by family composition. We're just part of the wonderful mix.

How are things going for Ben in middle school?

Even here in the San Francisco Bay area, middle school can be the hell years, so of course I still worry. I think Ben is learning how to stay under the radar, though, which is a good coping skill for any middle-school kid. It helps that many of his friends moved with him to middle school, so he has kids to eat lunch with, kids who don't give it a thought that he has two moms because that's the way it has always been. It's the kids who haven't known us since preschool or elementary school that worry me; will they find out and hassle him?

Have things gone differently with your second child?
Not really. They're so close in age; it's like we're all in this together. It still feels more like we as a family keep "coming out," rather than the kids having to do it on their own. I imagine that, later, when they're high school age maybe, college age definitely, they'll be more on their own when it comes to telling people about our family.

We have noticed, though, that our kids have had to make subtle adjustments that other kids haven't. For example, when I've heard them talking on the phone to friends, they'll use our first names. Instead of saying, "I'll ask my mom," they say, "I'll ask Kathy," or "Pam wants to talk with your mom." It's so they can distinguish us to people outside the family. I still love it when one of them says, "I have to ask my moms." I don't know why, but I just love how that sounds.

Do you make an effort to include men in your sons' lives?
We don't really have to; the men have just shown up. The boys have an uncle nearby who loves to play inane, violent computer games with them. And lets them steer his Ford Mustang when he's driving! He also rides bikes, throws the baseball, and plays

music with them. My partner and I do these things, too, but we can't lift them up and toss them in the pool like my brother can. Both kids have had male soccer and swim coaches. And their friends' dads have been wonderful role models, too, exposing them to heavy metal music, letting them race go-carts down the street—without helmets, of course—and run around a campground with sticks on fire, things that two moms would probably never let them do.

But the day I picked up Benjamin from Electric Car Camp and watched him drive the vehicle he and his buddies built around and around the parking lot—his hands dark gray, a smudge where he wiped at an itch under his nose, his Giants cap on backwards—I knew that it was all out of our control, anyway. Nothing we do will get in the way of their becoming men. They're both turning out just the way they're supposed to.

What About Rob?

Alex Munroe

Bicycle shorts. It all started innocently enough with a pair of bicycle shorts. How did it come to this? How did I become one of them? Was it revenge for all my years of working in a male-dominated environment, running circles around the nearest set of underqualified gonads and getting paid less while the 'nads go golfing with the mucky-mucks? Was it the margaritas? Or, when opportunity knocked, was I just as bad as they were?

After years of panty-hosing my way up the corporate ladder, I accepted a job as editor and moved to a small college town on the West Coast. To say I was a stranger in a strange land is a vast understatement. But to fully understand my dilemma, it's necessary to recognize the environment in which it occurred.

This town was an acquired taste. All at once, I was trapped in a funky haze between upscale yuppies and Cheech and

Chong's *Up in Smoke*. My first day of work was a doozy. Within minutes, a colleague asked me if I was a vegan. By lunchtime, I was walking down the main drag with another coworker as he pointed out the homeless, telling me their names in turn: "That's the spitting guy. That's the swearing guy. And stay clear of her; she's the farting wench." Some images you never forget, and to this day, I'll never understand barbecued tofu on a stick.

After the first year, having endured more than one round of musical employees, ours became an office led by seven female managers. Unfortunately, the boss—a creature with the grace of Medusa and the personality of a bar stool—spent three weeks out of the month PMSing and the fourth week apologizing. To say it was tense is being kind.

By then, I was editor of two magazines and helped manage the weekly newspaper. I shared an office with the newly hired newspaper editor, a wonderful woman named Gillian, a gal gifted with a quick wit, infinite intelligence, and a penchant for fine wine, cocktails, and chocolate—a woman after my own heart. Staff meetings were hideous, but we had each other, and that gave us the strength to survive the daily bouts of dictatorial ravings.

With work piling up and Medusa forever slithering down our backs, it became obvious that we needed to hire another writer. "Hire a local," Medusa hissed.

Panic set in.

We lived in a place where tie-dye was current fashion and people held candlelight vigils for Hendrix and Joplin. A place where hummus was the ambrosia of the gods and lentils were considered proper hors d'oeuvres. *You really want someone local?*

So with extreme reservation, we ran an ad and waited. Within days, we were flooded with letters, the majority of which read:

Dear Gentleperson,
I am amused by your search for a writer. I, myself, am an amazing writer and will consider your offer. I do not, however, believe in resumes because I feel they reveal too much information of a totalitarian nature and only serve to jade the minds of the unenlightened. I would be happy to meet with you, assuming of course it doesn't cut into my hot tub time.

The more letters that arrived, the more cabernet and Godiva we consumed.

After several weeks of being labeled everything from communists to Marxists to perpetrators of covert CIA ops, we received a letter from Rob. It wasn't particularly well written, but he didn't say "gentleperson" and he did include a resume—albeit slightly wrinkled—but a resume nonetheless. We called him in.

As interview day arrived, Gillian and I, in our sharpest power suits, waited for Rob. We'd been through plenty of industry interviews and were prepared with the standard queries for potential employees. As the scheduled time came and went, we chuckled and reached for another box of truffles. "Guess he needed more hot tub time."

It was just then that, out of the corner of my eye, I spotted a cyclist rounding the corner and parking his beater wheels in front of our window. Dressed in a bright yellow Lycra shirt and black bicycle shorts, he disembarked and stood tall. He was in his thirties, with a dash of curly brown hair and a Davidesque form. He carried a Pee-Chee folder.

Gillian was already ogling out the window.

"Can't be," I said. "Who the hell carries a Pee-Chee folder?"

"He's got a nice ass for a human bumble bee."

"Down girl," I said.

He was led into our office.

"I'm Rob," he said, beads of sweat glistening off his manly forehead, his bicycle shorts leaving nothing to the imagination.

Stunned silence.

"And so you are."

He sat down. And as the interview progressed, it was obvious that Rob, while sincere and friendly, hadn't a clue about the newspaper business. *But damn, he did have nice biceps.*

"What are your future plans?" Gillian politely inquired.

"Well, tonight, I'm going to the movies. Dunno about tomorrow."

I stifled laughter with a cough. "You want to be a career writer then?"

"Hadn't thought about a career," he smiled. "I do like poetry."

No way. I thought. *No poets.*

"Do you own a hot tub?" Gillian said sweetly.

"Actually, no. Is there one here?"

"Well, Rob, it was lovely meeting you," I blurted out in order to avoid a howl of unbridled hilarity. "We'll be in touch."

With a smile and a wink, he left, and we watched out the window with lascivious interest—not a word passing between us—until at last he pedaled beyond our view.

"He can't write worth a damn," I mumbled.

"I know," said Gillian, her eyes still focused on the horizon.

"He's cute," I said.

"I know."

"Margarita?"

"Absolutely."

Ten minutes later, we were seated at a Mexican joint, a pitcher of margaritas in progress. We pondered the obvious pros and numerous cons of hiring Rob, which sparked a lively debate—one that all males come up against on a fairly regular basis, but one that I faced for the first time in my career.

I was all too familiar with the male concept of hiring attractive females over more qualified males, but it never occurred to me to commit such a sin. Individuals stand on their qualifications, not their facade. Office eye candy? Never.

With tequila in hand, Gillian and I discussed various experiences we'd had being interviewed. I told her of a former boss I had and how, every time he spoke to me, he stared directly at my chest and how embarrassing it was to register that complaint with personnel.

"Ours is a sex-obsessed world, but we can certainly sleep better at night if we have a strong sense of morality," I asserted. "We can't hire the guy. He's not qualified."

"No, we can't. It's not right," she giggled.

By the second pitcher, we explored how perhaps our initial reaction to Lycra-man was unfair and that it was possible—with careful supervision—that he could become a reasonable writer.

After all, someone once gave us that chance, and you have to start somewhere, right?

"Okay, so we hire him for his potential?" Gillian smirked. "He'd still be high maintenance."

By the third pitcher, we reverted to behavior akin to that of cavewomen.

"The guy's got pecs from here to Milwaukee," Gillian mused. "And those legs!"

"Makes you jealous of the bike seat, don't it?"

By the next morning, I was back in the office, slightly hung over, but with my morals intact.

No way I'm doing this, I thought. *No way.*

As Gillian arrived, Medusa slithered in with her usual reptilian aplomb. "So, what about Rob?"

Gillian grinned, daring me to answer. Medusa hissed impatiently.

Not gonna happen, my brain screamed. But then I froze. *There are myriad forms of power in this world, but it's never been the norm for a woman to be able to exert power equal to a man in the professional environment,* I thought. *But there is today.*

"We're gonna hire him," I said. "Though he lacks experience, we feel that with training he could be . . ."

". . . a valuable asset!" Gillian said.

Medusa murmured something about payroll and slithered back under her rock.

Gillian grinned. "It was the shorts."

"Yep."

We then toasted our corruption with a pair of cappuccino truffles.

And so it was that Rookie Rob entered our funky editorial existence. He never could write worth a damn. And, on occasion, I'd lament over the time spent correcting his nonsense. But at the end of the day, I'd smile, knowing that his hiring gave me a glimmer of satisfaction.

Every woman should have a Rob at least once in their lifetime. For me, it was a pinnacle moment that in some small measure offered a bit of payback for all the leers, sneers, and "sweeties" I'd endured. You want to hire me to stare at my chest? I've got two words for you: bicycle shorts.

To a smart girl men are no problem
they're the answer.

Zsa Zsa Gabor

Alex Munroe is a veteran journalist, graphic designer, and author. A publishing "lifer" and self-proclaimed adventurer in humanity, Munroe spends her time researching and writing fiction and screenplays. She lives in the Pacific Northwest with her better half and five highly opinionated four-legged children. She is currently at work on a novel.

Who lasted longer with the company, you or Rob?

I lasted several years in that particular prison and then broke out. Medusa's incessant hissing and the burning need to expand my writing horizons sent me on a new adventure. I daresay Rob did continue to work for those publications for a while and, to my knowledge, has continued his writing career. It thrills me to know that perhaps we did give him a solid jumpstart.

What did you take away from that experience?

Hiring Rob was a show of power in a business where only the most tenacious and patient individuals survive. For my own growth, I needed to exert that power just once, even if it was exacting a bit of revenge on all the leches I'd come across in my travels.

Did you ever go out socially with Rob?

Our entire team of writers went out socially, including Rob. Although we spent fifty to sixty hours together during the work-week, we genuinely enjoyed each other's company. Besides, we were slave labor; so in the name of survival, we often combined our groceries and ate together.

If faced with that same decision today, hire a good-looking but unqualified male, what would you do?

I can say without hesitation that I wouldn't hire someone without qualifications. That was a one-shot deal. The many individuals I've hired since then were all chosen for their experience. Of course, no one since has showed up to an interview on two wheels, dressed for the Tour de France.

A Turn in the Right Direction

❀

Mary Laufer

If my husband had reported a water leak, I'm sure the landlord would have taken his word for it. But Mr. Edenfield heard my shaky voice at the other end of the phone and undoubtedly figured a woman didn't know what she was talking about.

"Never had a water leak over there before," he said.

I paced in the kitchen with my hand over the mouthpiece, muffling cartoons in the living room. Looking out the bay window, I had a clear view of the swampy lawn.

"The ground is just saturated from all the rain we've had," Mr. Edenfield explained. "The water pools in the low spots."

Nothing I said convinced him. I hung up the phone feeling like I'd been to a doctor who dismissed my symptoms as being all in my head. Mark always took care of household problems, but now that he was deployed, I was on my own. If I gave up without a fight, I could have a $300 water bill at the end of the month.

So I called Public Works. "Someone needs to check our water meter now!" I insisted.

Half an hour later, a pickup parked next to the curb, and two men in overalls got out. They tromped over to the green oval plate in the front yard, and the older man lifted it off the hole in the ground. With sweeping movements of his hand, he bailed out the water in the hole. Both men crouched down, their wide backs to me.

"We can't find anything wrong," the older man finally said. "The meter is barely moving."

"Then where is all the water coming from?" I asked.

He stood up. "There's something else I can try," he said and walked back to his truck.

I stared down at the water meter. A little triangle turned inside a circular glass case that looked like the face of a clock. Below the triangle, small numbers revolved very slowly like a car odometer.

The man returned holding a gadget with dangling wires. He knelt beside the hole.

"Anything running in the house?" he asked. "Washing machine? Dishwasher?"

I shook my head.

He took a stopwatch out of his pants pocket and glanced between the watch and meter. He'd attached a new counter with larger numbers.

"That triangle is spinning pretty fast now, isn't it?" I asked. "Can you tell how much water is leaking?"

He pressed in a button on the side of the watch, pulled a notepad out of his shirt pocket, and wrote down some figures. "Two-and-a-half gallons a minute."

"A minute?" I gasped.

The younger guy was investigating near the bay window. "Hey, Bruce!" he hollered. "Come here." He stepped down hard on the muddy ground with his work shoe, leaving an imprint that rapidly filled with water.

"There's nothing we can do," Bruce said to me. "The leak is in a pipe running from the meter to your house." He offered to shut off the water, but I didn't know how we'd live without it, so I told him to leave it on.

After the men drove away in their truck, I came to my senses. Two-and-a-half gallons a minute. It was as though the kids were flushing the toilet over and over. Now, thanks to me, a new meter was under there registering the lost water with perfect accuracy.

Mr. Edenfield promised to send a plumber in the morning. "The City workers shut off the water, didn't they?"

"Yes," I lied. It never occurred to me that the water had to be turned off before anyone could work on the pipes.

I called Public Works, but the office had already closed. At first, I felt like crying. Gradually, I began to see myself as capable, not helpless. How hard could it be to turn a little valve down in that hole?

When the kids were in bed, I collected a flashlight, an old coffee can, and a wrench from my husband's toolbox in the garage. I marched outside and aimed my flashlight at the oval plate. Running my fingernails along the edge, I clawed at the rim, trying to get enough leverage to lift the cover off. It wouldn't budge. I pounded it with my fist. The men had made this look easy.

I ran back to the garage, found a screwdriver, and used its flat blade to pry up the cover a few inches. The metal lid hung at an angle for a second, but it was heavy and it fell back into the hole sideways, splashing in the water and slamming into the new meter with a clank.

I hope I broke it, I thought.

Squatting down with the flashlight in my lap, I pulled out the lid, dunked the coffee can into the cold water, and emptied it repeatedly. As the waterline receded, the meter became visible through the murky liquid, the little triangle still spinning around and around, the numbers turning steadily. Layers of paper-thin leaves clung to the connecting pipes, and I brushed them aside, exposing the round shutoff valve. I adjusted the size of the wrench opening, and with both hands on the wrench, I gripped the valve.

"Lefty-loosey, righty-tighty," I whispered, repeating what I'd heard my husband say.

Every muscle from my shoulders to my fingers was flexed, yet the valve wouldn't move. Suddenly, I lost my balance and fell forward on my knees. The flashlight rolled off my lap, and its beam shot across the grass.

My jeans were soaked now, a mosquito was buzzing around my ear, and I could feel raindrops on the back of my neck. Lightning flashed in the distance. That's all I needed. I was going to get struck by lightning with my hands on this wrench in the water hole. Before long, it was pouring. The hole filled up so quickly that the valve was underwater again. My hair was drenched. The last straw was seeing my son holding the front door open and his sister jumping around beside him wailing, "Mom-meee!"

Let all the water in the world run through our meter, I thought. *I can't deal with it now.*

After the kids were back in bed, I sat at the kitchen table in my bathrobe and sipped hot chocolate. Rain hit hard against the window. The lacy curtains reminded me of the night Mark drilled holes to hang the rod. He'd had just enough time to set us up, and then he'd had to leave.

My palms were indented with pink marks from squeezing the wrench, and I'd somehow scraped a knuckle when I fell. I folded my arms on the table and lay my head down. Although I'd failed to turn off the water, I thought, *I'm thirty-three years old, and I am turning on a new part of me.*

In the morning, I lifted my head slowly, wondering why I'd been sleeping at the kitchen table. The sun was an orange glow behind the trees. The new day gave me fresh hope, despite the long stringy worm in the dirty water at the bottom of the hole. I hadn't seen the arrow on the valve in the dim light the night before; now it was clear. This time I knelt on a stack of dry newspapers so I'd be steady; and without the flashlight to hold, I had more freedom to move.

The valve turned. A quarter turn, that's all it took. The triangle stopped moving. But a shallow pond surrounded me. How would the plumber find the leak?

His name was Gibbons, and he arrived wearing wading boots held up by suspenders. I told him about the two-and-a-half gallons a minute and led him to the bay window. He shuffled around, his thick eyebrows bunched together.

"Yes, ma'am," he said. "There's a busted pipe someplace. Could be right here under the house." He mumbled to himself that he'd dig under there as far as he could reach, but he might have to go through the floor inside.

"Through the floor?" Furniture would have to be shifted, carpet pulled up, concrete shattered. I'd have to make a major decision without Mark. Move everything out of that part of the house? Break my lease and move out altogether? I'd just unpacked the last box.

Mr. Gibbons dragged his shovel to the front lawn, stomped on top of it, lifted the dirt out, and cast it aside. He dug several trenches near the bay window while I paged through the classifieds. We couldn't afford any of the rentals, much less the cost of movers. Yet my biggest concern was the kids; they'd be transplanted again when they were almost to the point of accepting this place as home.

Mr. Gibbons worked on the pipes for hours. He rang the doorbell at three-thirty, mud smeared on his nose. "Want to see what was cracked?" he asked.

I followed him out to a maze of ditches.

"Here it is," he said, holding a short plastic tube.

It was hard to believe that something so small had caused all the trouble. We looked down at the section of pipes he'd been working on. He said he'd glued the new piece and it needed to dry for three hours before Public Works turned on the water.

It was beginning to get dark when I carried the screwdriver and wrench out to the meter, popped off the cover like a pro, and turned the valve. There was a gurgle and then a gushing noise, and the triangle started whirling faster than ever.

"Something's wrong!" I screamed.

I kept my eyes on the dirt mounds, expecting a geyser to shoot out between them. Then I glanced back at the meter. The triangle stopped spinning. Completely stopped. That sound had only been water rushing through the empty pipes. I laughed so loud that echoes filled the neighborhood. I danced around triumphantly in the wet grass, waving the wrench in the air.

I'm not afraid of storms,
for I'm learning how to sail my ship.

Louisa May Alcott

Mary Laufer grew up in East Aurora, New York. A military wife, she moved with her husband from state to state, attending five colleges along the way and earning a BA in English from SUNY at Albany. Her essays and poems are published in Learning to Glow, a Nuclear Reader *(University of Arizona Press, 2000),* Proposing on the Brooklyn Bridge *(Grayson Books, 2003),* Hello, Goodbye *(July Literary Press, 2004), and* Hunger Enough: Living Spiritually in a Consumer Society *(Pudding House Publications, 2004).*

What did your children think of their "new" mom?
I think my son felt more secure knowing I could keep the household running. My daughter was too young to understand, but since then I've been a good role model for her.

Where was your husband deployed?
My husband wasn't allowed to tell me exactly where he was going because of the nature of his job. He is home with us now.

What was his reaction when you told him this story?
At first, he was a little amused. Then he questioned why I didn't look in the telephone book to see if there was an emergency number for Public Works. He said I was lucky because in the end, at under $100, our water bill wasn't as high as it could have been.

Did he notice your transformation?
He noticed that I borrowed his tools to fix things around the house, and he was peeved if I didn't put them back exactly where they were before! I didn't even see them as his tools anymore.

Have you tackled any household projects since?
Yes. Everything seemed to break when my husband was deployed, and I didn't have my father or brothers to depend on because I was far from home. I took apart my front doorknob when the deadbolt stuck; I used the wet-dry vacuum to suck out a plug in our air conditioner; I even made a minor repair on my car. Sometimes I asked for advice, but I never waited for a man to fix anything anymore. I tried to do it myself.

Fishing with Men

❧

Jennifer Kocher

It's early morning, and we're driving down Seward Highway, the 127-mile stretch connecting Anchorage and the Kenai Peninsula. The sun is muted behind a wall of purple and brown clouds, creating a bruise along the upper ridge of the Turnagain Arm. Terri has the wheel. She is my boyfriend's brother's new girlfriend. Our boyfriends are driving in front of us, pulling the boat. Their elbows poke out of the side windows, forming small, flightless wings.

Terri and I have failed at small talk, so I move on to personal questions: *Are you close to your family? Do you like your father? Are you happy in Alaska?*

She responds with short answers: *More or less. Sometimes. I have my days.* And soon the conversation hits a lull.

The only thing I know about Terri is that she is an archaeologist whom my boyfriend finds "exquisite," which I find a bit extreme. Diamonds are exquisite. Sunsets on white-sand

Caribbean beaches. The *Mona Lisa.* But a woman with small, deep-set eyes, who digs up skeletal remains?

I watch the exquisite archaeologist pop an orange peanut butter cheese cracker into her mouth. She has boy-length hair and a tall, lanky body. She stares at the road with a stern expression, reminding me of the humorless aunt that I always seem to find myself sitting next to at weddings.

She asks me if I've fished much, and I shake my head, unwilling to admit that I'm here for my boyfriend, not for the fish. I'm not exactly the outdoor type. I wear velvet, and I grew up in the suburban Midwest where I spent my free time in malls, piercing my ears and shoplifting lipstick.

Terri's backseat is full of complicated-looking gear, so I assume she's serious about fishing, at least enough to dump some money into it. She tells me that she's been trying to catch a salmon all summer. I stare at her blankly. I've never had a female admit that to me without irony. The last girl I went fishing with showed up with a thermos full of margaritas and a book. The women I know are like me. Their boyfriends have outdoor obsessions, and they've developed a tolerance so they can see them on the weekends. We've taken a vow of incompetence: We good-naturedly endure the activities, but we don't have to be good at them.

Terri follows their truck down the windy gravel road to Canyon Creek. We park, and the opening of the doors initiates a whirlwind of activity. Everyone is doing something, rifling through trunks and bags, zipping, snapping, carrying. I stand off to the side like a lost child.

My boyfriend, Matt, hands me a large, blue jumpsuit and tells me to put it on. Because I don't own a single piece of equipment, I'm used to wearing oversized items. But this thing has a hose. When I point that out, he tells me that I can use the hose to inflate the hood if I fall out of the boat and sink. *Perfect.*

Terri walks toward the boat, and I do a double take. She is wearing thigh-high waders, which look incredibly sexy over her jeans. My oversized suit, formerly cute by right of its hideousness, now makes me feel completely inadequate. I feel like some girly-girl attempting and failing to be G. I. Joe.

Matt's brother Danny motors the boat downstream while Matt and Terri sit together on the middle bench, assembling their rods. I watch them and smugly determine that, from this angle, *they* could be brothers. After all, they have the same hair, short, floppy, brown. Yet her hands are thin and delicate, purposely moving in a way that makes fishing seem artful.

I'm suddenly eager to fish, so I tell Matt that I am dying to catch one, *absolutely dying.* He gives me an amused smile and continues discussing tackle with Terri. I listen intently, ready to leap into the conversation at the first recognizable word: *hook, line, sinker.* After a few minutes of language-barrier alienation, I decide to do something proactive. I roll up my sleeves into large donuts and lean over the side of the boat, scouting for any moving shape in the water that remotely resembles a fish. The trouble is that I have terrible astigmatism and keep mistaking rotting leaves for salmon.

It's Danny who spots a school of salmon, so we anchor under an alder bush. As I watch their dark, slippery shadows disappear under our boat, I start to feel a warm rash forming at the base of my neck in what I assume is an adrenaline rush. I chew my nail and wait for Matt to finish assembling a rod, wishing I had paid attention one of the hundred times I've watched him do it so that I could take it out of his hand and expertly finish the job.

Matt hands it to me and offers a few quick casting lessons, pointing to dark spots in the water where he says I'll find fish. I hurl the line over my shoulder, and my hook almost hits Danny, who ducks just in time. I apologize and try again, this time forgetting to open the bale so that my hook lands with a splash right in front of me. Matt laughs and shakes his head.

I hear Danny compliment Terri's casting style, and I glance over to watch the graceful arc of her line as it sails into the water. She keeps her rod still and parallel to the horizon line. I give myself a pep talk. *Not only will I catch a fish before her, but I'll catch the biggest fish, one worth mounting. I can see it now, its silvery lacquered body forever frozen in a giant leap over my boyfriend's mantel.*

Terri reels in and gets ready to cast again. I watch her movements—rod casually resting behind right shoulder, left hand over right, with grip on reel, right arm pivoting, rod horizontal to body, hook landing fifty yards away in water—and try to mimic her, move for move. Her line hits the water, while mine snags the alder bush. I feel myself starting to lose it.

The last time I remember trying to be good at a sport and failing so miserably was on the soccer field my junior year in high school, when girls dribbled circles around me. Years later, I understood this meant I was a mediocre player. At the time, however, I saw it as other girls trying hard to make me look bad, which prompted me to act in the only way that my stunted maturity allowed: I kicked their shins.

"Great cast, Terri," I say in a phony voice.

Matt looks over at me with a puzzled look, as if trying to put his finger on my tone.

Terri looks over at me and smiles. I know that smile, the same smile you give to someone in a wheelchair: *I am able-bodied and guilty about it.*

"You're doing great," she says, giving me the thumbs-up. Then she turns to Matt and asks him if he thinks she would have better luck using such-and-such fly.

"I wouldn't have thought so," he says, "but I think you might be right since the water's so high."

I hurl my line until I'm sweating. I notice that Terri has taken off her fleece jacket and is fishing in a tank top, so I unpeel my suit and slip out of it. The icy air invigorates me, and I unsnag my line and try again. Matt stands behind me, coaching me. It's the most annoying thing in the world, and I wish he would just shut up and move out of the way.

Danny makes a whooping sound, and I look over to see Terri fighting with her rod. Danny dances behind her, shouting for her to keep her line away from the motor.

"I'm trying to," she yells, stumbling to get under his outstretched arm. Her rod is nearly bent in half, and the veins stick out of her forearms.

I will her to fail. I wish her line would break or, better yet, she would fall out of the boat and sink, her waders ballooning with water. As if to spite me, she maneuvers the large black-and-white fish to the side of the boat where Danny waits with his net. He lifts the net into the air.

"That's got shoulders," Matt says with admiration.

The fish flops around on the floor of the boat, its bloody gills opening and closing like car vents.

"Nice work, Terri," I say, wishing the fish would stop flopping and just die.

She pulls the hook out of its mouth and sticks her fingers into its gills so she can lift it in the air for Danny to take her picture. It thrashes around while Danny digs in the bag for her camera. It's starting to make me sick. I'm a loser, yes, but that's not what's bothering me. It's the fish's spastic convulsions. As I watch it die, I can't believe that I was trying to kill something for the sake of my ego.

"Aren't you going to keep trying?" Matt asks me.

"No," I say. "I'm done."

• • •

Terri and I ride home in silence. I don't even attempt small talk because I no longer care about her fish or that my boyfriend finds her exquisite. I do something that I never would do in front of my boyfriend. I complain about being cold, tired, and hungry. After I say it, I wait for her to laugh and roll her eyes and tell me about the night she survived in the woods by eating pinecones.

Instead, she turns up her heater and makes a sharp right into a gas station parking lot.

"Let's get some food," she says. "I'm starving."

We walk under the fluorescent lights to the snack aisle. I hear a high-pitched laugh, and I turn to see a gaggle of wet-haired teenaged girls in bikini tops walk through the front door. The girls make a beeline for the soda machine, shoulders touching as they fill their cups with Diet Coke.

I'm embarrassed, feeling the way I always feel when I'm caught in the company of somebody else's good friends, jealous of their friendship, stuck outside their intimacy. I feel the urge to turn to Terri and make a joke or tell her a funny story about my best friend. Something to prove that we are having fun, that we aren't just two very different women with nothing to talk about.

If I were standing in this aisle with my best girlfriends, I would grab anything deep-fried and salty and not think twice. I resent Terri as I pass the Pringles and hover in front of the nuts, looking for something unsalted and marginally healthy that won't make me feel any worse about myself. I grab a bag of sunflower seeds and hold them up for Terri.

"How about these?"

"I was hoping for Doritos," she says, leaning down to grab the large bag, and I suddenly marvel at her self-confidence.

"And jelly beans?" I say.

"Definitely." She smiles at me.

Some days, I look for signs of my own mental development, some tangible proof that I've matured beyond the petty roles that ruined my teenage years. Other days, I understand the futility in believing that age equals maturity and instead realize that we're driven by our own survival instincts. Our need for self-preservation brings out the very worst in us.

The girls stand in front of us in line as we wait. I stare at their tan, chicken-bone backs. Two of the girls whisper together while the third one flips one of their ponytails, leaning over her shoulder, saying, "What? What?"

Terri grabs the candy out of my hand and puts it on the counter, elbowing around me so that she can pay for it. I don't fight and peacefully stand behind her as she digs into her wallet.

As we drive, I eat a handful of Doritos and comment on the fact that our disgusting junk food is the perfect accompaniment to the foul odor of her salmon. She laughs and admits that she's not sure why she wanted to catch one so bad.

"I don't even really like salmon," she says, scrunching her nose, which until now I hadn't realized was small, almost delicate, almost feminine.

We want the facts to fit the preconceptions.
When they don't, it is easier to ignore the facts
than to change the preconceptions.

Jessamyn West

Jennifer Kocher has a MFA in fiction from the University of Montana and is completing her MA in creative writing at the University of Colorado. She won a 2002 AWP Intro Journals

Award in creative nonfiction and CU's 2004 Jovanovich Imaginative Writing Award for best graduate manuscript. She is published in the Mid-American Review *and* Georgia State Review. *Originally from Ohio, Jennifer lives in Miles City, Montana, with her two cats and two pigeons.*

Are you still in touch with your fishing companions?
Matt and I are still together, but I never saw Terri again after that day. Matt's brother broke up with her shortly thereafter.

Have you continued your pseudo-outdoor exploits with Matt or any other men in your life since the time of this story?
Living with an avid hunter and outdoorsman who relegates his life according to hunting seasons makes it nearly impossible for me to avoid going on outdoor exploits. That said, we've been together long enough now that I feel much more confident saying no. When we first started dating, I did everything, from hunting turkeys, deer, and elk to once camping in the snow in search of bighorn sheep. Now, I usually go on one hunt a year, this year for turkeys, which I enjoy. We're also planning to go find morel mushrooms and wild asparagus this spring, two of my favorite foods.

Have you found any outdoor pursuits that you now call your own?
No, but living with Matt has opened my eyes to entirely new pursuits that I would never have found on my own. For example, last year, I had two pet pigeons that we kept in a coop in

his backyard. I used to think that pigeons were flying rats whose sole purpose was to humiliate city dwellers by pooping on their heads. However, after our first two pigeons were mutilated by a cat that had snuck into their coop, I was devastated and insisted that we get two more. I even went with him in the middle of the night to find them, holding the ladder and net while he snatched two squabs out of a nest in an abandoned, downtown building.

Ever go fishing again?
Yes. In fact, now I love ice fishing, as well as fishing for perch and bluegill in the summer. I'm in it mainly for the fish fry at the end of the day, but I found that I also like the thrill of hooking and reeling in the fish. I still can't bring myself to touch the bait or unhook the fish from the line; but fortunately, Matt doesn't seem to mind doing the dirty work.

Coming Out

✤

Jamie M. Pearson

I am a preternaturally precise person. I shelve books by subject, organize my junk drawer weekly, and rotate my socks. I cannot walk through a room without adjusting pictures on walls, refolding towels, and lining up spice jars. In my weird little world, there is only one right way to load a dishwasher, the person who uses the last of the dental floss is morally obligated to write it on the grocery list, and very few pots and pans actually need to be soaked overnight.

Some people might call me controlling.

I have never been spontaneous. I believe that major events in life are too important to be left to chance. My husband Rich and I met at twenty-five and married at twenty-seven. By my calculation, this was the perfect age. We were old enough to choose intelligently but young enough to enjoy being newly-weds. Our picturesque June wedding was choreographed down to the last canapé, boutonnière, and slow dance. We rented the perfect apartment and furnished it to my exact specifications. I chose a large dining room table for the frequent dinner parties I forecasted hosting and a compact sofa bed for the inevitable houseguests.

My plan called for us to spend the first five or so years of our marriage pursuing careers and hobbies and the next sixty-five being parents. We bought a house, acquired a dog, and traveled. A few months before our fifth anniversary, I threw away my birth control pills. One month later, I was pregnant.

I had always planned to love pregnancy and approached the venture in this spirit. With my usual attention to detail, I kept a journal, made lists of baby names, interviewed obstetricians, and researched strollers. I shopped for maternity clothes, read books, did Kegels, and tested eleven shades of interior latex flat yellow paint for the nursery.

This kept me very, very busy.

So busy, in fact, that I was three months pregnant before I finally slowed down enough to notice that I was feeling a little lukewarm about my expectant state. I still wanted the baby but realized I would probably prefer to accept delivery via stork or UPS.

At first, I denied it. It wasn't pregnancy that didn't agree with me per se, just the nausea and fatigue of an unpleasant first trimester. This was to be expected, I reassured myself. I'd probably be back on board in just a few weeks.

But then I didn't like the second trimester, either.

Or the third.

Pregnancy was just not working out the way I'd planned. I enjoyed my baby's first gentle nudges, but the subsequent round-the-clock acrobatics were literally gut-wrenching. I liked the idea of seeing an ultrasound image of my unborn child, but the extraterrestrial eyes that stared out at me were unnerving. I gained fifty pounds. I cried all the time. I grew a beard.

At precisely twenty-seven weeks gestation, I decided to revise my plan to be radiantly happy during pregnancy. The new plan didn't call for me to revel in pregnancy, just survive it. This solution was elegant in its simplicity and pleased me tremendously. As I opened a pregnancy book and skipped ahead to the chapter on childbirth, I felt lighthearted for the first time in weeks.

Curled up with my dog on the couch, I read all about the different stages of labor. I scrutinized a cross-section of a pregnant uterus and pored over a list of common complications. I studied a frightening drawing of a fetus presenting in breech position and memorized the steps to take during an emergency home delivery. Each time I turned the page, my horror grew. A gruesome photo of an infant's crowning head sent me running to the phone to sign up for childbirth classes.

The classes were held at the hospital in Berkeley where I planned to give birth. It was a plush, private facility known as the best obstetrical center in the area, and I had chosen my obstetrician largely because she had admitting privileges there. But before my first prenatal class, I had never actually seen the inside of the building. As Rich and I entered the almost-holy hush of the lobby, with its sweeping high ceilings and imposing floor-to-ceiling oil paintings, I felt momentarily awed. It seemed more like a trendy modern museum than a medical establishment, and there wasn't a single sick person in sight.

We found our way to the classroom, where we joined eight other couples in a semicircle of folding chairs just as the class was beginning. The teacher was a middle-aged white woman dressed in a gauzy, sari-style dress. She flipped a long, graying braid over one shoulder and introduced herself as Phoebe.

Phoebe explained how to preregister at the hospital, outlined the key differences between false labor and real labor, and described some nebulous-sounding pain management techniques. As I recall, the big three were breathing, staring at a fixed object in the room, and hugging your partner and swaying. According to Phoebe, the pain of labor was bearable because it was productive. She told us contractions felt like menstrual cramps. When Phoebe disclosed that she had never actually *personally* given birth, I seriously considered asking for a refund.

That night, I called my best friend Anna for the real story.

Months had passed since the vaginal birth of her *eleven-pound baby*, but she had wisely remembered every detail with perfect, horrible clarity, just in case her husband ever suggested repeating the experience.

"It's more like being eviscerated with a Swiss-army knife while your body spontaneously turns inside out," she informed me. "On the other hand, it's not unlike being mauled by grizzly bears." Anna seemed to be enjoying my terrified silences just a little too much. "Did you ever have menstrual cramps like that?"

At the next class, I shared this frightening anecdote with the woman seated next to me. "Apparently, it's not like cramps at all," I whispered to her over a Dixie cup of watered-down orange juice during the break. "It's more like being stabbed repeatedly."

For reasons I still don't understand, the woman remained sanguine. Like most of our classmates, she was committed to natural childbirth. This blew me away. Why was painful childbirth considered such a badge of honor? *What about natural root canals,* I wanted to shout to this crowd of masochistic Madonnas. *How about natural appendectomies?* Instead, I bit my tongue and waited impatiently for Phoebe to cover anesthesia. When she did, it was almost a footnote.

At the end of the last class, Phoebe invited each of us to tell the rest of the students what we were planning. This was a big focus of the class: creating a so-called birth plan. Everyone spoke in turn. In addition to squeezing tennis balls and staring at clocks, the other women were mostly planning to suck on ice chips and listen to Enya while they waited for their babies to be born. If things really got bad, perhaps they would *take a shower.*

I thought they were delusional.

When Phoebe nodded at me, I glanced at Rich. He must have known what was coming because he was studying his shoelaces with great interest. I took a deep breath and outlined my plan. No matter what, I wanted to forgo the medieval pleasures of natural childbirth. I required an epidural and as early as possible. Next week would be convenient, in fact. The other couples laughed, but Phoebe just smiled tightly. It was obvious she thought my plan was tantamount to bottle-feeding my baby Diet Dr Pepper.

The months crawled by.

I stocked up on newborn provisions. I narrowed down the list of baby names. I attended a baby shower in my honor.

I couldn't stand being heavily pregnant but didn't want to go into labor, either. And yet as far as I could tell, there was no other viable way to get out of this. My pregnancy had progressed normally, so—even if I hadn't been embarrassed to broach the topic with my obstetrician—a scheduled C-section was out.

The nicest thing I can say about labor is that it made pregnancy look like an all-expense-paid luxury vacation. And I never actually went into labor. Labor overtook me. Labor completely possessed me. Labor threw me a two-hour blanket party. And it did feel like menstrual cramps. For about fourteen seconds. Then it felt like being stabbed repeatedly. Then it got worse.

I was brought up to be uptight about bodily functions. During my childhood, I cannot remember anyone ever speaking the word "fart" aloud. If it was absolutely necessary to refer to flatulence—and I don't remember that it ever was—the accepted phrase was "pass gas." We did not discuss menstruation. We did not talk through the bathroom door to another family member who was urinating. When I learned that many women inadvertently move their bowels on the delivery table while pushing, I nearly died.

Minutes into labor, it became obvious that I would have nothing to worry about on this front. This is because one of my first symptoms was explosive, intestine-cleansing diarrhea. From my station on the toilet, I made a strangled "AAAARRGH!" sound during each of my frequent, tightly spaced contractions. My labor hurt right from the start, and the pain never seemed to recede long enough for me to do more than gasp raggedly.

Once I felt certain that I was not going to faint right there on the toilet, I conducted various pain management experiments. When I closed my eyes, my contractions hurt more. When I dug my fingernails into my puffy kneecaps, they hurt less. When I bellowed like a bull walrus, they hurt even less, but this had the unfortunate effect of alarming my husband.

Each time I yelled, he would wait a decent interval and then softly call out, "Is it over?" I pictured him lurking right outside the bathroom door with a stopwatch. "Are you okay?"

I was not okay.

This went on for almost an hour. After a while, I stopped answering him to safeguard what little remained of my sanity. He became concerned and phoned my doctor. He forced the door open to hand me the phone, and the conversation went something like this:

The Doctor: How are you doing?

Me: Um, not great.

The Doctor: Can you talk through your contractions?

Me: AAAAAAAAARRRRRGH! (muffled splashing noises).

The Doctor: (without a trace of irony) That sounds productive! I think it's time you went to the hospital.

Me: AAAAAAAARRRRGH! (more splashing).

I wish I could report that this was the low point, but it wasn't even close. Next came the car ride of the damned. Although I had never seen Rich more sweetly solicitous of my comfort, I was never less comfortable in my life. As it turned out, the contractions were a thousand times more excruciating when I was sitting in the car. As he gingerly steered us to the hospital, he couldn't seem to shut up. Would I like him to recline my seat? Did I want the windows open or closed? Did I prefer classic rock or easy listening? Did it hurt when he braked? What about when he accelerated? Did I want a sip of water?

When we finally arrived on the maternity ward, we were directed to the triage area where a nurse asked me to step into the bathroom, disrobe, and pee in a cup. I have no idea why. Perhaps people who can pee in a cup aren't really in labor. Maybe they are sent home until things get worse.

I staggered back to the examination table shaking my head and clutching the empty cup. The nurse was in no particular hurry until she realized I was five centimeters dilated. Then she sprang into action. Five centimeters! We had to hurry to the delivery room. We needed a gurney, now! But none could be found on such short notice. With no small amount of embarrassment, the woman informed me I would have to walk.

I lost no time setting off on foot in nothing besides my thin, cotton hospital gown. Rich followed close behind with an armload of my maternity clothes. "Have the anesthesiologist meet me there," I gasped as I limped away barefoot. *"Please."*

The nurse just smiled and waved. "Good luck!"

I don't really know how I walked to the delivery room. In retrospect, it doesn't seem physically possible. At this point, I was in hard labor. I remember only flashes of this journey. Rich clutching my arm too tight. An older woman reading a book in the waiting area. While I was panting and inching my way down the corridor, we saw another pregnant couple. I presume they were pacing the maternity ward in an effort to jumpstart her sluggish labor. They were holding hands, looking cute and hopeful. The woman gave me a sisterly smile as we passed each other. Just then, a contraction hit, and I doubled over. I am not religious, but I screamed "Oh God! Oh Jesus! Oh SHIT!" through the worst of it.

The cute couple hurried away.

I think my superhuman strength probably had everything to do with the fact that I actually believed there was a chance the anesthesiologist would be waiting, needle in hand, when we arrived.

Finally, we found our room. As we walked in, our labor and delivery nurse smiled and introduced herself. I was astounded that anyone could do something so ordinary in the face of such obscene pain. In some remote region of my brain, it registered that she was from the South. Tennessee probably or maybe Kentucky. Her bedside manner was nice and easy. I could have killed her.

"Well, hi y'all," she said with a wide smile. "Aaaahm Nell."

"I'M . . . FIVE . . . CENTIMETERS . . ." I huffed. "AAAAAAARRRRRGH!" Thankfully for the hospital custodial staff, the diarrhea had passed by now. "Call . . . the . . . anesthesiologist."

Nell nodded but did not rush to the phone. My heart sank. It was obvious she thought we had plenty of time. Ever so slowly, she settled me into the bed and started an IV. Then she took my blood pressure and fitted me with an elastic fetal monitoring belt. With Nell making small talk the entire time, it was the longest fifteen minutes of my life.

I inquired about the anesthesiologist's whereabouts seven or eight more times.

Rich suddenly looked panicky. "The car!" he all but shouted. "I have to move it!" In our haste to seek immediate medical attention, we had parked in the ambulance-only zone in front of the emergency room.

I gave him a horrified look. How could he even consider leaving me alone with Nell? This was not part of my birth plan. It was then I remembered the camera. "Go!" I said. "HURRY!"

While he was gone, Nell finally deigned to check my cervix. "Let's jus' see how you're doing," she soothed. She waited patiently as I howled my way through another contraction and then reached inside me with a faraway look on her face. "You're SEVEN centimeters now." She actually said this as if it were good news. There was still no sign of the anesthesiologist.

A few astonishing contractions later, Rich returned with my overnight bag and found me almost catatonic. From a mute place of mind-altering pain, I heard him ask Nell to check me again. Nine centimeters! She broke the bad news to us with a smile—my labor was progressing far too fast for an epidural. We would be holding our baby before pain relief could possibly arrive.

For a moment, I just couldn't get my mind around this. Impossibly, the nightmare into which I'd been thrust was about to get worse. This was my first baby; I was supposed to labor for twelve hours. According to my books, labor was meant to start gently and intensify gradually. I was entitled to pharmacological pain relief if I wanted it. Firing out a baby in two hours with no drugs was not part of my birth plan.

My peripheral vision went gray and fuzzy, and I literally could not speak words. In one semicoherent moment, I remember thinking, "So this is what it's like to go insane." My contractions were continuous now. There were no valleys, just peak after peak after peak. Nell counseled me not to scream quite so much.

"Save y'energy foah pushin'," she said.

Save your bullshit for someone who's getting an epidural, I thought.

The birth itself was violently quick. All at once, I felt an unbearable pelvic pressure. I found my voice and struggled to describe the sensation, all the while fearing I was about to crap on the delivery table. Nell spotted the baby's head and rushed to call for reinforcements. Moments later, an unknown doctor ran into the room and scrubbed. The pediatrician joined us seconds later. Nell and Rich propped me up and held my legs, I pushed three times, and I was a mother.

As the doctor laid my baby girl on my abdomen, I blinked back tears of joy and relief. I felt an almost visceral surge of love for my daughter and not only because her arrival had been my own deliverance. I reached one trembling hand down to touch her. She was goopy and skinny and perfect in every respect. She was also screaming her fuzzy little head off.

We named her Avery.

At first, nothing in the delivery room met with Avery's approval. The pediatrician suctioned her tiny mouth and nose with a bulb syringe and treated her eyes with a goopy ointment. This pissed her off. I got to hold her for a moment, but then she went to the plastic bassinet to be weighed and measured. At last, Nell gave her a bath and swaddled her tight. Avery liked Nell about as much as I did.

When Avery was back in my arms at last, she scowled up at me for a long moment before settling at my breast. The birth experience had obviously left something to be desired for her, as well. Perhaps she had had a birth plan of her own. Overwhelmed by the instantaneous connection I felt to her, I drew her closer and pressed my lips to her furrowed, angry little forehead. Already we had so much in common.

As I held my daughter tight, the obstetrician announced her intention to stitch up my wounded perineum. I took stock of my situation and wondered aloud if it might be possible to have some narcotics now that there was a break in the action. As I swallowed the proffered handful of Vicodin and Motrin tablets and straightened the tangled blankets that surrounded me, I began to feel like myself again for the first time in months. With a smile, I adjusted my bed, asked for orange juice, and requested another pillow.

I was back in charge.

❧

If pregnancy were a book,
they would cut the last two chapters.

Nora Ephron

Jamie M. Pearson is a writer, mother of two, and U.S. expatriate. Her work has appeared in Parenting Magazine, Utne, Brain, Child, *and in the award-winning anthology* Toddler: Real-life Stories of Those Fickle, Irrational, Urgent, Tiny People We Love *(Seal Press, 2003). A native of northern California, she currently lives with her family in England, where she is working on a memoir about the dark side of motherhood and is launching a family travel Web site called* www.travelsavvymom.com.

How did the birth of your second child compare with the first?

After my ridiculously short labor with Avery, I shopped around for an obstetrician who shared my fear that I'd sneeze this second baby out while stuck in traffic or at the grocery store. I found a lovely doctor who agreed to schedule an induction, and still nothing went according to plan. In all the excitement of my record-fast dilation, the labor and delivery nurse forgot to turn down my Pitocin drip (the drug used to induce or augment uterine contractions). When the doctor didn't appear on time, I begged for—and got—more pain relief. I wound up nauseated, numb from the teeth down, and too wasted to follow simple instructions. To this day, I have no idea how my son Max was born.

How has your controlling nature fared now that you're the mother of two children?

Believe it or not, I still finish my Christmas shopping by September, glue my photos into albums on a regular basis, and floss nightly. Control is not really a choice with me; it's more of a disease.

What's life in the U.K. like?

Living abroad is the best thing we've ever done. From shoe shopping to crossing the street, literally everything is an adventure. Additionally, we're making every effort to wear out our passports traveling around Europe. Avery and Max have acquired many unexpected points of reference: Where is spaghetti from? What is the purpose of the Eiffel Tower? Why doesn't America have a queen? At three and five, they are so worldly that it scares me.

Your memoir sounds fascinating. Can you tell us a bit more about "the dark side of motherhood"?

The mother-lit publishing trend may be on the wane, but I think that there are still issues that need to be raised. What exactly does it feel like to repeatedly scrape feces out of your toddler's Hello Kitty underpants with a butter knife while in the throes of astonishing morning sickness? What is the correct playdate protocol when your three-year-old daughter and her friend find a tube of personal lubricant jelly in your nightstand drawer and covertly apply vast quantities of it to their faces and hair? What exactly does it feel like to discover that breastfeeding has made you permanently and conspicuously lopsided? And many more.

Hair Today, Man Tomorrow

Ginger Hamilton Caudill

Losing a breast or dying are grave concerns with breast cancer, but, to my mind, chemotherapy hair loss can trigger just as much emotion. My cancer support group explained that some people wake up to discover all their hair on their pillow. Others lose large clumps at inopportune moments, like while dining with an important client. I've been the class clown all my life and can appreciate a certain entertainment value in having a lock of hair plop into my soup bowl. On the other hand, I'd rather lean on my spoon with my elbow and have it sail through the air.

A few weeks into my first chemotherapy cycle, I found I could gently tug on my hair and it came out in my hand. It seemed my hair wasn't attached by its roots, but simply stuck to my head by static electricity. No one had told me about that phenomenon, and I found it creepier than the prospect of my hair dropping out en masse in public.

I got a few laughs out of reaching up, grasping clumps of hair in each hand, and declaring, "I'm just going to pull my hair out if you don't stop." Then I'd pull my clenched fists away from my head, and they'd be full of that weird static-clingy chemo hair. On an entertainment scale of one to ten, I'd give it a five—not really worth the trouble.

So I formed a battle plan. I could handle being bald for several months, but I wanted control over the time and place it happened. My oldest daughter would cover my scalp with intricate henna designs. I planned to bravely bear my bald badge of courage. My defiance would transform a symbol of sickness into a piece of art and blaze a trail for other women to go bare. I cut my hair very short, boy style, and waited for The Day.

One morning, my brush promptly clogged with clumps of loose hair as I groomed. It was time. I took a strip of duct tape and rolled it into a circle, sticky-side out, then ran it over my head till the remaining hair was gone. I still had a little fluff here and there, like some mangy animal, but that soon fell out, too. Making sure the bathroom door was locked, I used a hand mirror to check out the one external part of my body I'd never seen before—the back of my own head without hair. Unfortunately, my head is an ugly shape, with thick fat rolls that I didn't want to draw attention to with artsy henna designs. Who knew? Eventually, I left the privacy of the bathroom and faced first my family, then the world. My daughter agreed, decorating this monstrosity of a noggin would be like embroidering a car cozy—not impossible, but highly impractical.

Plan B, I traipsed to the cancer center's wig-lending library. There were more than two hundred wigs to choose from—

lovely long auburn falls, chic glossy black dreadlocks, and sophisticated blonde styles. Unfortunately, not only do I have an ugly-shaped head, it's gigantic, too. Surprise. Only two fit, both of them frosted, ash-blonde, old-lady-style wigs.

I chose one of the two old lady wigs that I could cram on my head and wore it three or four times. July heat and humidity combined with no air circulation under the wig created sores on my scalp, so I returned it. Maybe some big-headed old lady who shivered all summer long could use it.

Plan C, turbans. Now, turbans look odd without hair underneath to fill them out. To compound that problem, whenever I turned my head quickly, the turban didn't turn with it. There was nothing there to cause friction to hold the turban to my head. So not only did I have a big, ugly head with sores on it, but if I jerked my head too fast, I looked like a drunk with my turban on sideways. Finally, I discovered terry cloth and fleece turbans—these would hang on for the ride—and that is what I wore.

Tired from the treatments, I took a lot of naps that summer. One afternoon, I dreamt I had long, flowing, chestnut hair again. I ran across a field of daisies in slow motion. My hair bounced in the sunlight. I could feel it on my neck, against my back. Then I heard a *bang*. Another *bang*. I awoke. *Bang*.

I got up and tramped into the den to determine the source. Seven teenaged boys were tumbling about in various demonstrations of wrestling holds. My son and his friends were rough-housing just on the other side of the wall from my bedroom. Fourteen eyes locked onto me, and the teens all froze where they were, like they were playing Statue. Amazed at the respect

I'd commanded, I said, "Guys, you know I'm sick. This is my naptime. It's very important I get my rest, okay?"

They remained motionless and silent while I continued. "Please, cool the noise. If you want to wrestle, go out in the yard or down in the basement. But my bedroom's on the other side of this wall, and I can't sleep if you wrestle here. Get it?"

Every one of them nodded, but not a word was spoken. Every eye remained fixed on me. It was all I could do not to break into a happy mommy dance. I had total power over these guys. Now for the coup de grace: "Any questions?"

Eric raised his hand. Eric never talks. He's a great guy who goes through life chomping on Honey Nut Chex Mix and smiling a lot. Once, I overheard him speak an impressive three sentences when he told the new kid in the neighborhood, "Mrs. Caudill will feed you any time you ask. It might look like dog crap, but it always tastes great. She don't let nobody go hungry." Other than that one touchingly candid occasion, the only words I'd ever heard Eric say were "Thank you."

I was impressed. If Eric was speaking, this had to be important.

"Yes, Eric?"

"What happened to your hair, Mrs. Caudill?"

The boys' rapt attention wasn't because of my imperious commands or their deep respect for me. Nope, they were in shock seeing me bald for the first time. I'd forgotten to put on my turban when I stumbled out of my bedroom.

I mumbled an explanation, repeated my request for quiet, and slunk back in my room to nurse my pride.

After that, I chose not to wear the turbans at all. I figured nothing could be worse than that fiasco.

I was wrong again.

My husband and I went shopping one afternoon not so long after the living room debacle. I enjoyed getting out of the house, but my endurance and energy level were lower than I realized. Exhausted, I asked him to bring the car to the front of the store while I paid for my items. After he left, I waited in line at the checkout counter. When my turn came to pay, the clerk looked at me, smiled, and said, "Cash or charge, sir?" I was half asleep, and at first, I didn't realize she was speaking to me. She looked me right in the face and repeated her question: "Cash or charge, sir?"

How could she think I was a man just because I had no hair? What about my curvy figure, my elegant hands? I let the last strand of pride about my appearance go. This was her problem, not mine. I knew who I was despite anyone's perception of my external self. Invisible doors to the universe opened at that moment. I was no longer tied to someone's idea of what I should look like. I was a woman, fully realized, vulnerable and strong.

Literature is strewn with the wreckage of those who have minded beyond reason the opinion of others.

Virginia Woolf

Ginger Hamilton Caudill worked for many years as a nurse before returning to her first love, writing. Her work has appeared in numerous publications, including storySouth, The Front Porch, Mountain Echoes, Dead Mule, USA Deep South, and Any Dream Will Do Review. *She presently lives in Charleston, West Virginia and maintains a Web log at* http://chicken scratches.blogspot.com. *Ginger also writes a monthly advice column for* Penwomanship Magazine.

How has your experience with cancer changed your perspective on life?

The physical changes from my cancer treatment remind me that beauty truly is on the inside (thankfully). It's best appreciated through action and not observation. I follow my bliss now. I figure we're all leaving this planet feet-first no matter what we do. Goals are fine, but don't miss out on today's joys.

I've learned humility. It isn't important to be in control of everything. I'm more forgiving of myself and others. I've gained a healthier perspective into my own spiritual weaknesses and strengths. I've learned to cherish the small pleasures of life—piping hot rolls fresh from the oven just dripping with butter, and the way my arm smells when I've been outside in the sun. I've learned to relax my standards. The world doesn't come to an end when my ten-year-old goes to school in a wrinkled uniform, for instance. And so far, the School Laundry Police haven't issued a warrant for my arrest (although charges may be pending). In November 2004, I felt strong enough to pursue my lifelong dream of publishing my writing. Currently, I'm logging ten to twelve hours a day at the computer.

How is your health today?
I'm five years out from the original cancer diagnosis. Recovery was draining and took much longer than I expected. I eat better quality foods now, cut back on fats and refined sugars—just like everyone else! The biggest change is that now I respect my body's signals and nap when I'm tired. As of my last examination, the cancer's in a state of suspended animation. I encourage it to rest as long as possible.

Being Elmo

Kendra Alvey Parsons

My blonde wig itched, and I felt sweat rolling down the back
of my costume. I hoped the kids wouldn't notice. It was swel-
tering, and I was sick of everyone looking at me. I needed to
get paid so I could get the heck out of Dodge. I spotted the
father across the room talking to two other dads. I made my way
toward him, reminding myself that the sooner this guy paid up,
the sooner I was home free.

"Excuse me, sir. That'll be one hundred dollars."

"Sure, Sugar. You know, you're a lot cuter than the girl we
had last year." The man leaned closer to me and made a pathetic attempt at a wink.

He handed me six twenties and elbowed the sloth next to
him. "Cowgirl Barbie. Next year, I'm getting Malibu Barbie again.
She wears less, dude. But, Cowgirl Barbie does have that lasso."

I heard them laughing as I shoved the cash into my jeans,
grabbed my games and face paints, said the obligatory goodbye

to the birthday girl, and ran outside to the driveway. I waited until I'd driven around the bend to remove the heavy wig and cowboy hat. Wouldn't want any little girls realizing Barbie's not real, would we? I grabbed a baby wipe and removed the heavy foundation that was supposed to make me look like I was made by Mattel.

As I drove down the 101 toward home, I gratefully shed bits and pieces of my costume. If the neighbor guys saw me in one more embarrassing outfit, I was sure I'd commit suicide. They seemed to find something sexual about every character. Their favorite was Alice in Wonderland. They would rush after me, blabbing something about rabbit holes and a Cheshire cat smile. At first, I tried being a smartass back, but it's hard to maintain your dignity wearing knee socks and carrying a balloon pump.

I reminded myself that at least Cowgirl Barbie looked seminormal without the wig and hat. Maybe I could squeak by unnoticed by the perverts. I made a pledge to drop off resumes the following day. I needed a real job. Real money. I wanted to spend my weekends shopping at Barneys, not dressed up in his purple suit.

The truth is, I moved to Los Angeles with the same delusions every other hometown heroine has. I planned to walk down the red carpet in Valentino, not trip over tricycles in a Rug Rats head. How could I not be getting auditions? They loved me in West Texas. So, to support myself, I'd joined the humiliating bottom rung of the acting ladder. Well, maybe not the absolute bottom. I figured the guy dressed up like a Subway sandwich on the corner was lower than me. But I had a sneaking suspicion he made more.

Children's birthday parties. It seemed like a good idea at the time. I only worked when I wanted to so I could take off for auditions. Not that I had many. Plus, tips were involved if you got lucky, and hey, I loved kids. I'd failed to realize what I was doing to myself. The word *humiliation* comes to mind. So does the word *lost*. I was terrible at directions, so the act of driving to some far-off location like Northridge dressed as a clown and trying to look up highways in my *Thomas Guide* made me want to slit my ruffled throat.

But I could fit into the smaller costumes, so Head Clown often let me play the better roles. I was usually spared the horror of the clown suit or the sheer terror of having to wear a heavy hollow head simply because I could fit into Beauty's dress and the Little Mermaid's tail. Which was no picnic either. Try running after thirty toddlers when you can only take baby steps because of your fin. I was once tackled by a gaggle of unruly children whose parents were taking turns at a beer bong. It took me a really long minute to stand up again. I wish I could say that was the most embarrassing it ever got.

It wasn't.

There was the time I posed as the Easter Bunny. I wore the white head and the furry costume with the hands cut off so I could make balloon animals, a skill I now use only at Lakers games when I'm sitting behind the goal and I've had too many $10 beers. The head was so big that it went past my chest. I couldn't see anything without scrunching my neck to my shoulders and peering through the mesh eyes, which hit around my chin.

In the middle of the party, an eager mother shoved her kid at me and requested a picture. The child was chanting, "Eat the bunny! Eat the bunny," which I found disturbing considering I was roasting hot. I blindly groped around the area surrounding my knees and found the little body waiting to be picked up. I grabbed the eloquent toddler under her arms, pulled her upward to rest on my fuzzy hip, and promptly banged her head against the hard bottom of the bunny head. I was rewarded for my efforts by a high-pitched scream. No one else wanted their picture made with "Eat the Bunny" so I spent the rest of the gig accidentally stepping on Easter eggs in the backyard. Good times.

My humiliation reached fever pitch when I was hired to play Elmo at a Montessori school. The day before, I'd been Snow White, and I still had the red fingernails. I was pretty sure Elmo was a boy and didn't have long, red nails. I hoped no one would notice. Head Clown reminded me that Elmo always referred to himself in the third person. As I approached the classroom, already sweating in the stinky costume, I thought to myself, *Elmo is out of here in an hour. Elmo is making her beer money!*

Apparently, there was a step going down into the classroom. Probably anyone not sporting a large red Elmo head would've seen it. As I tripped and stumbled into the enormous room, I heard a roar of giggles. A grating, high-pitched mess of mockery. There must've been fifty kids sitting cross-legged on the carpet, anxiously awaiting their victim.

The teacher patted me on the shoulder and walked out the door carrying a pack of Marlboro Reds. "See you in an hour, Elmo."

I panicked. *Was she going to leave me alone? With them?* I told myself that it would be fine. I could handle this. Elmo would conquer. We played the parachute game without incident. I taught them the good ol' chicken dance. Then, it happened.

I was making a balloon sword for a rowdy little man of a boy. Between grunts and shouts of "Charrrrrge!" the child watched my hands intensely. As I presented him with his blow-up weapon, the boy yelled, "Elmo's a girl!"

It became a chant. "You're not real. Elmo's a girl. You're not real. Elmo's a girl."

The children became wild, crazy beasts, running around the classroom and doing Elmo knew what because Elmo couldn't see anything. I backed up, bumping into one of the little chanters. I spun around, trying to get my bearings. "Please calm down for Elmo," I begged.

The brats became a pack. The sword fella emerged as their leader. He yelled, "Get herrrrr," and the herd complied. I was pushed and tackled. Grubby little hands pulled my tail and attempted to de-head me. I moved as fast as I could, tripping over toys and cursing the teacher inside my head of torture. No fair. Running in an Elmo costume is like skiing with a garbage can on your head.

It's hard.

It really is.

I don't know how long I ran around the room. I found out later that Montessori schools don't believe in strict discipline. I've found that I don't believe in Montessori schools. About the time I was ready to pull my red carpet-head off and scream that Santa, the Tooth Fairy, and your first love aren't real, the teacher reappeared with a check and Marlboro breath.

It was the lowest I'd ever felt. I'd been spooked by a bunch of four-year-olds. I was a hot, sweaty pathetic Elmo. I'd broken a nail, I didn't get tipped, and I couldn't stop crying. The sobs echoed inside the head, making me feel like I was in a cave of sadness. My dream of a nice sit-com career was distorting into a deranged fun-house reality. And my performance didn't even get canned laughter. I was pathetic. I was a twenty-four-year-old college graduate, and this is how I was forced to make money? What was I going to say back home in Texas at Christmas when people asked me how things were going in la-la land?

I imagined myself sitting in Chili's saying, "Oh, it's great. Totally great. I work all the time."

I finally located my car. I reached up to take the heavy, furry, smelly head off at last. This was when a car full of teenage boys drove by and yelled, "Tickle me, Elmo!"

Elmo hated herself.

I drove home, devoid of all red fur, wishing I'd bummed a cigarette off the teacher. I saw an old lady leaving a restaurant in my neighborhood. She waved good-bye to her friends and slowly made her way down the sidewalk. She wore a content smile on her wrinkled face. I wondered what she'd done with her life and if she'd ever been humiliated. If she'd ever had a job she hated. It dawned on me that she probably had. That everyone has. But, there she was, old and wrinkled and smiling like she'd just won the lottery. I realized that if I survived the drooling herd of Satan's breed, I could survive anything.

After using several colorful words to curse four-year-olds, I couldn't help but giggle. If I were four, I would've tortured me, too. Picking on Elmo is funny. Maybe being Elmo would be funny, too, if I could learn to laugh at myself.

I parked my car by my apartment, put on the Elmo head, and strutted through the courtyard to my place, relishing the laughs and applause coming from the boys on the porch.

Okay, I was Elmo. A terrible Elmo. So what?

Now, when I take life too seriously, I think about Elmo. And I don't hate myself.

I told her I would play a Venetian blind, dirt on the floor, anything.

Whoopi Goldberg

Kendra Alvey Parsons is a twenty-nine-year-old recovered actress residing in Los Angeles with her husband, Tim, and their cat, Dixie, who recently changed her name to Mrs. Nice Nice. Kendra graduated from Southwest Texas State University in 1997 with a BFA in acting. She has written a novel, several short stories, and children's books, which all reside in a file marked "stuff" on her laptop. They hope to someday be read by others. Kendra is hard at work on her second novel.

How did the acting pan out?

My favorite acting coach, the late Larry Hovis, always told me that if I could do anything else besides acting and still be happy,

then I should do it. I had an epiphany after an especially grueling series of auditions to play a princess on *Mighty Morphine
Power Rangers*. I ended up losing out on the role, and I realized
that I loved to act but hated to audition. Actors audition ninety
percent of the time. Therefore, I was miserable ninety percent
of the time. I discovered it just wasn't for me.

Do you think you'll ever go back to it?
No. I know I made the right decision when I stopped pursuing acting. I don't miss it. I love to write, and I don't have to
audition for the privilege of sitting down at my computer every
morning. When my best friend landed a role on a major night-
time drama and I wasn't at all envious, I knew I would never
regret my choice. I do, however, keep my SAG (Screen Actors
Guild) dues current because you never know what I'll want to
do when I'm an old lady. I may be jonesing to do a Depends
commercial.

**If you could turn back time and arrive in Hollywood
again, would you do anything differently?**
I'd like to say that I wouldn't have moved to Hollywood in the
first place. That I would have stayed in Texas and been writing
right away. But I'm glad I moved here. I learned a lot and I met
my husband.

**If you met a young woman who was headed for Holly-
wood with stars in her eyes, what would you tell her?**
I would tell her to develop a thick skin, to be ready for loads
of rejection. I would also encourage her not to take it all so

seriously. It's a business like any other. Auditions are not life or death, and casting directors want you to do well. If you see it as a job and not a dream, you'll be better off. I would also tell her to be true to herself. A major agent once told me that I was cute, but not sexy enough. He said I should come back the next day looking as hot as possible. I had my hair and makeup done, wore stilettos, the whole shebang. He took one look at me and shook his head. At the time, I felt like a failure, like I wasn't good enough. I've since realized that I should have found an agent who was willing to market me as cute instead of trying to make me into something I wasn't.

Life on Neverland

✧

Sarah Bowman Zale

We sailed out of San Diego in December on a thirty-six-foot ketch, her course written plainly on the stern: *Second star to the right, straight on till morning.* Her name, *Never Neverland,* flowed in a flourish across a teak ribbon.

I sailed with my new love, Michael. To cruise was his dream. After thirty years of working for IBM, he had looked for a way to answer a call from the sea. We'd filled a storage unit in Colorado with furniture, skis, and winter clothing and moved to San Diego.

I knew nothing about boats when we first set eyes on *Neverland.* The storyteller in me found her name enchanting. The bright teak throughout exuded a homey feeling. I thought the eight-by-ten-foot aft cabin cozy, with its sink and double bed, and the angled floor a curious challenge. Peter Pan, Wendy, Michael, John, and Tinkerbell frolicked in a painting on the stern in a fantasyland where dreams never die. Although I knew nothing yet about where we would sail or what it would take to get there, the romantic in me nodded my approval.

Michael worked about the boat from early morning to dusk. I stopped asking the particulars of his chores because his explanations completely eluded me. I attended a few seminars and scanned the sailing magazines for how-to hints. Words such as *ohms* and *bandwidth* became part of my vocabulary as I studied for my HAM radio license. I read sailing books, such as Tania Aebi's *Maiden Voyage,* full of unimaginable terrors about a young woman circumnavigating the world alone. The words of these women sailors intimidated me.

I was hitchhiking on Michael's dream and unworthy of the label *sailor:* "Tweaking the sails" to assure they were operating at peak performance didn't thrill me. I watched the sea surreptitiously from the corner of my eye. I didn't trust it; yet I yearned to understand it. Its power and mystery both engaged and terrified me. I eventually went cruising in spite of rather than because of what I knew about sailing.

At midnight, ten days after we first set sail out of San Diego, whipping seas twisted our anchor, ripped off one of the flukes, and then cast us out to sea. We sailed for twelve hours into the next anchorage. Bahía San Carlos rested calm upon our arrival. We anchored in the lee of high rolling hills and fell asleep at sunset. The anchorage curved around us like a letter "C" about to close.

Furious rocking woke us in the middle of the night. The anemometer, which registers wind velocity, indicated twenty-five knots. Even veteran sailors cast a worried eye to whitecaps rising in a protected anchorage. Wary about heading to the open sea, we waited. Within the hour, the winds escalated to thirty. *Neverland* shook. We felt like seeds in a rattle. In an effort to ease the stress on the anchor line, I started the engine and butted the head of *Neverland* into the wind. When the anemometer skipped to forty, the wind whipped the sea into foam. A fifty-foot trawler, not far from our stern, called out by radio, "My anchor chain has snapped. I'm heading to sea."

Michael shied away from the question in my wide-eyed stare. *What power could pop a chain built to hold a twenty-five-ton yacht at anchor?* We considered following the trawler's lead, but it was too late to safely straddle the bow and raise the anchor. Clad in foul-weather gear, we huddled in the cockpit against the damp cold as the needle of the anemometer repeatedly threw itself at the maximum reading of sixty. Santa Ana winds came at the nose of the boat from mysterious places within the hills and arroyos of the anchorage. The anchor held onto *Neverland* as if she were a kite about to catch the whip of air that would whisk her to the sky. Swells rose like a huge cat, pounced on the bow, then exploded against the windshield of the cabin. With every attack, we ducked our heads and winced.

"Monitor our position," Michael yelled over the howl of wind against sea. He took the wheel.

I turned from the storm to watch the sky, its steady light of stars impassive to the chaos below, and monitored our position by the stars. If Orion no longer peered over the port stern, his belt holding us steady, I would know the anchor had snapped and we were headed for the rocks.

Hours passed. We said little. Prolonged terror has a way of dulling the senses. I thought about death. I searched through my memory for any regrets, finding them in the area of love more than anyplace else. Michael loved me. I knew that. Yet I had always doubted if I was loveable. More than that, I feared I was incapable of loving. It occurred to me that stormy night, I'd gone sailing with Michael because I believed him capable of ending my doubts.

The three bright stars along Orion's Belt hypnotized me. I recalled a scene from the movie *White Squall*. The final moments between the skipper Sheldon and his wife Alice played out in my mind's eye. Alice lies trapped in the brigantine ship *Albatross* as it sinks on its side. Sheldon, having exhausted all attempts to rescue her, watches her, his face accepting, his eyes in searing anguish. Her look is the same. He touches the window she cannot reach. I sense the fullness of his loss because I have seen them as a team, sailing their vessel out of one danger after another. I ached to become lost in such a love.

I looked at Michael and wondered if there was any greater proof of love than to know I felt peace to die at his side. I was where I wanted to be. It wasn't my dream to go cruising, but it was my wish to spend my life with someone who supported and nurtured my dreams and who believed my presence gave his own dreams greater meaning.

All at once, waves tangled on the port side, then exploded into the cockpit. I knew if I were thrown into the water, I lacked the strength to elude the snare of the waves. At best, I would tread water, then slip into senselessness from hypothermia and drown. My imagination watched it happen.

I know how Michael thinks. "Promise me," I whispered, "that you'll save yourself. I'll be fine." He steeled his gaze and looked away. Minutes, perhaps hours, passed as the storm blasted around us.

"Are you afraid to die?" I asked.

He looked straight ahead to think about it, then shook his head with a slight twitch as if to say: *This is not the time.*

The high winds continued through the night. We never moved from our places in the cockpit. Michael stared at the bow, hanging onto the wheel as if he believed he could save us. I gazed into the serene sky and escaped to other places. Although snuggled in sweats and waterproof gear, I shivered. Michael, always the caregiver, offered me a sleeping bag. I slipped into its cocoon.

"By daylight, it will stop," I assured him, wanting to give something in return. I drew from an untapped place within, confident not about boat engines and riggings and anchors, but about an inner strength beyond muscle, a strength women often have in higher reserve than men.

By 10:00 A.M., the wind had eased somewhat. Michael worked to raise the anchor. The chain had broken free of its cleats and rollers. We found no way to bring it in. Michael cut the rope connecting us to the chain and anchor while I powered the motor against a wind still eager to push us to the rocks.

It was a mistake. We should have known better. The rope whipped with Poseidon's fury into the sea and lassoed the prop, disabling the motor.

Somehow, we managed to raise the staysail and sail into a sea of six-foot swells and inexorable wind. We had lost the motor and two of our three anchors. The jib had unfurled and ripped loose. Michael suggested we return to the port of Ensenada.

"No," I said.

The image of paper signs hastily slapped on five boats in Ensenada reared up in my mind. The owners had posted them the morning after arriving from a hazardous journey down the U.S. coast. The scrawled messages said, "For Sale." The words meant, "I quit!"

The autopilot no longer functioned. Hose clamps now attached the boom that had separated from the mast. Exhaustion made our movements slow and calculated.

"We're halfway to Cabo San Lucas," I told him. "Why go back?"

He looked at me oddly for a long while, then smiled the kind of smile a guy gives another guy while planning a fishing trip or having a beer during a football game. I smiled back.

We continued on into the persistent high winds and swells. On *Neverland*. In search of paradise. It's what sailors do.

It is good to have an end to journey toward; but it is the journey that matters, in the end.

Ursula K. Le Guin

Poet, biographer, and freelance writer and editor, Sarah Bowman Zale teaches writing online from her Web site, www.sarah write.com, and in the university setting. In 2003, after sailing throughout Mexico, she moved to her current home in Washington state. Her poem "if the moon, if you dance" prefaces

the memoir By the Grace of the Sea: A Woman's Solo Odyssey Around the World *by Pat Henry (McGraw-Hill, 2003). Her poetry has appeared in* Comstock Review, Sow's Ear Poetry Review, Wind Publications, WomanMade, *and others. Whether writing poetry or prose, she believes in the poetic word to both honor and change the world.*

What happened after you continued to sail with the damaged boat?
In a bit of a stupor, we sat with *Neverland* at a work dock in Cabo San Lucas, waiting for repairs. Eventually, we pulled ourselves together and headed north up the coast toward La Paz. We never made it, of course! Thirty or so miles later, we hit a storm that held us two weeks in an anchorage called Los Frailes. After that, we went directly east and made it to Mazatlán.

Was that the end of your journey?
No. We sailed south down the coast of Mexico over the next four years. During hurricane seasons, late spring to fall, we would settle inland in Ajijic, south of Guadalajara. Ajijic is the largest expat community—primarily Canadian and American—in the world. I've heard it said that once a sailor gets salt in her veins, she loses the sense to say no to the sea. That seemed to be happening to me.

When you weren't suffering through storms, what was sailing like?
Of course, there are the perfect days of sunshine and eighteen-knot winds, the ones you see in movies and in sailing magazines,

but they're actually quite rare in Mexico. To understand most of our sailing experience, picture your home as a small, narrow closet with a kitchenette. Add your husband or partner and a slight rocking. Imagine yourself there for hours, then days. Do you hear the waves against the hull? Hear the clock ticking? Listen to the quiet. The wind. The waves. The ticking.

I see that Michael sometimes trusted your judgment despite your lack of sailing experience. How is decision-making normally handled onboard ship?

Michael was the captain, which means I agreed to let him make all final decisions while underway. I was documented on the crew list as the pilot. If the captain became incapacitated, I had the official authority to sail the boat alone. Designating a captain is critical to the sailing process because you need someone to make the split-second decisions. Democracy doesn't work. So that's how it was on paper. Reality was this: After receiving an order, I would run around saying, "But why? Why?" Bottom line, though, Michael and I learned a lot about compromise and support. It's typical that cruising with someone either seals the relationship or breaks it. There's no in between.

Have you had any epics at sea since this adventure?

Oh, too many to count! And I'd like to add that a woman's sailing story is typically different from a man's. Men tell of "perfect storms." Women sailors speak of what all women talk about in general: their fears of being controlled, incompetent, and unloved; their joys that come from relationships that work; and the realization of an inner strength that comes with challenge.

The Missing Mother/Wife Link

❧

Anna Grace

My mother-in-law had not been in my house ten minutes when she assured me that, while nursing her fifth child, the milk flowed so hard, she'd grown a third nipple, but not to worry, over the years, it shrunk down to the size of small mole—and would I like to see it?

To her credit, it did feel longer than ten minutes since the dilapidated camper bearing Darlene and Jud had rolled into our driveway, a puff of smoke signaling its death. All the way from Mississippi they came, to help me with their newborn grandson, Ben. A child that quickly began fretting in my arms because it had been, what, forty minutes since he'd last eaten?

"Excuse me," I said, sitting on the sofa and reaching up under my silk blouse to wrestle with the hooks of my nursing bra. Ben, sensing food was forthcoming but not yet in his belly, really began to wail.

"Now, Momma, you'd better jump to it," Darlene said. "I can see that child has you at his beck and bidding. 'Yes, Momma,' he says. 'I'm hungry. I want some of Momma's good steak and potatoes.'"

I smiled briefly at this keen observation of my child's hunger, finally settling for unbuttoning the top of my blouse, as I could not get those stupid hooks to unfasten.

Now, I'm the sort of gal who likes to do something right if she's going to do it at all. Breastfeeding Ben those first few weeks was never right. He would get hungry in an instant, complain intensely, and after less than three minutes of nursing, he'd get distracted and turn his head, while mother's milk continued to flow freely. I'd try to coax him back, but some new fascination would always arise, resulting in frustrating, milky interludes that pretty much filled my days. Now I had an audience.

Jud stared in absolute fascination; the tension between a woman baring her breasts and the absolute perversity of milk flowing out of them had him mesmerized.

"Ummm, Momma, he likes that," Darlene commented.

I didn't respond.

"Ummmm, Momma, good."

My eyes flicked over to my husband, Mike, whose face had gone gray.

"Umm, Momma, good, nice. Ummm. Momma. Oh, oh, yes. Steak and potatoes. Umm. Good," she continued to chant. The entire time I nursed him.

Then I'd gotten the third nipple story.

It was around that time that Mike declared he needed a new pair of pants. My husband owns three pairs of Levis, one pair of khakis, and the black bottoms to the suit he married me in. He shops for pants once every five years. Yet moments after his mother's arrival, Mike was in his truck headed to the mall, leaving me at home with his mother and her fourth husband. He may have had a valid reason at the time, but by now, it completely escapes me.

Jud and Darlene looked at me. I looked at them.

"So," I said, having tucked my mammaries back into my shirt, "Jud, are you from Mississippi originally?"

I knew he wasn't, but I figured we could have a nice, little geographical conversation with that starter.

Nope. Twenty minutes later, Jud was still answering my question, with ". . . Now my ears had been swelled up for years, ever since I was a boy, and they always dripped. Dripped and dripped. Got so bad that my neck swelled up clear out to my shoulders. My ears, they were dripping something awful. I went to the doctor, a nice dressed man, suit and tie. He said he'd have to lance it. Now that hurt, a sixteen-inch lance, sharp as a hound dog's spare tooth. Well, he lanced my left ear, and all that fluid in my neck and ear came flying out, just flying out, and covered that doctor in his nice suit and tie. The smell of it could launch a buzzard off a shit wagon . . ."

The horror of Jud's ear appeared to be over, but like the residual dripping, I was to be "delighted" with this story and many others, again and again.

Each day was a blur as I fixed meals, did dishes, cared for the baby, and drove my in-laws back and forth to Napa Auto Parts, all to the soundtrack of Jud's stories and Darlene's commentary on the inadvisability of the frontpack their grandson was necessarily tucked into. The stress was worsened by the fact that I was waiting for an important call from my boss regarding the possibility of a part-time assignment after my maternity leave.

When Mike finally did walk in the door, I would thrust the baby into his arms and announce that dinner was really complicated and it would be best if no one interrupted me while I made it.

The strangest thing about this whole episode is that my husband is a really loving, generous, family-oriented guy. As one of five children raised by a greasy-spoon cook and . . . Darlene, Mike is an American success story. He's brilliant, well-read, a true craftsman, *and* he can cook. And he was completely AWOL during his mother's visit. I was about to kill him.

Thursday, Ben and I skipped out on the second daily trip to Napa Auto Parts to visit a friend "in crisis." Ben was an angel, cooing and gurgling while Molly not only made me a cup of coffee, but also offered to hold the baby. I stayed late, chatting and laughing at the expense of others.

Just as I was wrapping up a description of my in-laws' wardrobe, Molly said, "Isn't it funny to think that most men marry women similar to their mothers? I can't imagine how you're like Darlene." And she smiled, like that really was funny.

I went home.

I can't say I expected dinner to be simmering on the stove and Mike ushering his parents out the door to a movie when I returned, but I certainly didn't expect the scene that awaited me. The house was a mess, Jud was talking, and my husband was lying on the sofa with his eyes closed.

"Can I help with dinner?" Mike asked.

"No," I snapped.

Jud glanced at my chest.

"Looks like yer leakin'," he commented.

The wetness along the front of my blouse needed no confirmation from my father-in-law. I sighed.

"Yes, Jud. I am leaking."

I strapped Ben into the frontpack and headed into the kitchen.

Annoyed at everybody, I banged around making dinner, every burner on high. Ben began to fuss, so I opened the front of my blouse and used one hand to hold his head so he could nurse while I cooked. Pork chops were still leaping in the pan long after the spinach had finished steaming. I didn't care if dinner was half cold or half burnt. I didn't care about anything.

"Honey?" Mike called from the living room. "A couple of people called for you."

"Who?"

"They're on the message machine."

I left the chops scorching and walked over to the phone—nothing.

"There are no messages," I told Mike.

"I must have erased them."

"Who called?"

"I can't remember."

"There were two messages, and you can't remember who called?"

He lifted his arm from over his eyes. "I think one might have been Angela. The other was a woman . . ."

"My boss?"

"I don't know."

I stormed into the living room. There I stood, baby in frontpack, shirt open, breasts streaming milk while Ben had a peek about, dinner burning on the stove. I stared at Mike, then dropped the spatula on the coffee table and walked out the front door.

Quickly, I took my precious son to the most remote corner of the yard. I sat under a plum tree, too frustrated to cry. Who did Mike think he was? *Jerk. Scum Bag. Monkey Butt.*

"Sweetheart?"

I didn't look up, just stared at the hem of Mike's new pants.

"Look, honey, I'm sorry about the phone calls."

"This isn't about the phone calls. It's about . . . ." I paused; I didn't even know where to begin. "You know, that might have been a really important phone call."

He sat in the grass next to me and cupped his face in his hands, rubbing at the day's stubble. "I didn't mean to erase them. It's just that Jud was talking and—"

"Jud was talking? Shocking. I'm shocked."

"You don't have to make fun of them."

"And you, apparently, don't have to be around them. I work for them all day. Your mother has never, not once offered to take the baby. Or offered to help cook."

"Maybe that's because you—"

"Because I what? Now it's my fault I have to do everything?"

Mike turned to look into my eyes.

"You can be a little difficult to help sometimes," he said quietly.

I was so angry I wanted to hurl something, but the only thing in my arms was little Ben, who I happened to like.

Mike was still talking. "My mother doesn't like to make mistakes, and you can be kind of particular. You have some pretty rigid standards. Mom probably doesn't feel real welcome."

"How can you say that? I go to the auto parts store twice a day."

"Anna, you know what I'm talking about."

I began to rip out a neat patch of grass.

He was talking about the fact that I'd rather put the dishes away myself than reput them away after someone had done it wrong. He was talking about the fact that I'd put him in remedial laundry training a month after we were married. He was talking about the fact that I'd held maybe three babies before having one of my own, not because no one trusted me with them, but because I wasn't exactly sure how to do it right.

He was talking about the missing mother/wife link. Darlene was a perfectionist. Which would explain how she managed to raise such a great guy and why she was hesitant to help, particularly after that time I pulled the whisk out of her hand.

It still didn't explain Jud, however.

"I know I've been a real jerk this last week . . ." Mike started.

"And a Scum Bag and a Monkey's Butt."

"I have a hard time with Jud." He looked up into the branches of the plum tree, all the angst of one's mother marrying such a man moving through his face.

"So you leave it to me to entertain him? Do you know about the ear story?"

"I'm sorry," he said, turning to gaze down at Ben. I placed the baby in his arms.

"I need more than sorry right now."

Darlene either had some sixth sense advising her about our conversation or she'd been listening from behind the gardening shed, but when we returned to the house, the blackened pork chops had been covered over with some sort of gravy and the cold spinach was creamed beyond all recognition in the traditional Mississippi way. It's not what I would have made for dinner, but hey, it was really good.

The next day, Mike stayed home from work. And as the visit stretched on, Mike spent more time at home, holding Ben as Jud's endless stories lulled the baby to sleep. There were even several days my husband went so far as to work on the camper with Jud so Darlene and I could have some story-free time together.

For my part, I did my best to see Darlene not as a houseguest with a broken camper, but as the woman who raised the love of my life. As I relaxed, she relaxed. She even strapped on the frontpack a few times and agreed it was pretty handy. Humor and good sense were not traits my husband had pulled out of a vacuum. Darlene displayed an abundance of both in dealing with a somewhat—do I want to call myself prissy? I suppose I must—a somewhat prissy daughter-in-law and her baby.

Two weeks after that fateful Sunday, Mark watched bemused as Darlene and I loaded up the camper. There's an art to it, you know.

"You girls need any help?" he asked.

"No," Darlene snapped.

Mark caught my eye, grinning. I smiled back.

"The mother/wife team has got it covered," I told him.

"Yeah," he said, "I bet you do."

All perfect in the camper, Darlene and Jud piled in. With tears in our eyes and smoke rolling out of the exhaust pipe, my in-laws headed back to Mississippi.

I come from a family where gravy is considered a beverage.

Erma Bombeck

Anna Grace lives in Coburg, Oregon, with her family. She teaches high school history part-time and writes when her children are willing to nap.

Have you and Darlene visited since the time of this story?
We now talk frequently. She's a real kick, and Mike and I have tried to keep in closer touch with her. When I found out I was expecting our second child, I called Darlene and invited her out for another visit. She'll be here this summer. I'm really looking forward to it, but I am going to make sure that Mike has all his pants shopping done before she arrives.

Is Darlene still married to Jud?

No! Somewhere in the midst of one of his endless stories, Darlene suggested Jud and his camper put-put on out of her life, and she's much happier for the loss of him.

How is your relationship with your own parents?

I am so lucky when it comes to parents. My folks divorced and remarried when I was quite young. Now all four of my parents are good friends, and all of them love Mike. Mike and my stepdad are particularly close. I think this was part of the problem with Darlene's visit. My family is so tight; she felt like an outsider. She wanted to help me with Ben but, at one point, found four other grandparents there, hovering around their first grandbaby. This next visit, I hope my folks will get to know Darlene for the cool lady she is. I mean, if my mom can enjoy shopping with her ex-husband's second wife, surely she'll come to love her new partner-in-grandmothering.

Funeral for a Live Ex-Husband

Ellen Sommers

Once, I had a bulldog named Clyde. He was a brindled, bomb-shaped animal whose favorite toy was my son's socks. Seeing the rolled-up ball of white cotton on the floor, Clyde would seize it in his cavernous jaws, and no amount of coaxing would convince him to let go.

Once, I had a husband named Herb. After we wed when I was a teen and were married for twenty years, he left me for Barbara, a quiet homebody of a woman whom we had both known for several years. Finding it difficult to let go of the idea that I would be married forever, I shook and throttled the dead relationship until it was as limp and ragged as my son's socks in Clyde's jowls.

I've heard it said that resentment poisons the vessel that holds it. If that's true, then I was a walking toxic waste dump. One night, while playing nostalgic seventies music, I beat my hands on the sofa in uncontrolled rage. The next morning, my palms were as purple as irises. I wrote Herb a letter enumerating all of his sins, making sarcastic reference to "bread-baking, mustard-making, husband-taking Barbara." I wrote a nasty poem in the form of an Irish curse, part of which wished that his male member would shrink to the size of a leprechaun's finger. Obsessed with his new relationship, I tortured myself with the fact that he'd had an affair with Barbara while he was still married to me, wondering if he had made love to both of us on the same day. I felt vindicated when my children reported that she served gummy rice, gritty dip, and bloody Cornish game hen at a preholiday party.

My only solace was when, every day at school, I would spend a common forty-five-minute break with my friends, Jane and Karen, who listened to me take my ex-husband's inventory, listing his sins like out-of-date, swollen cans of Campbell's soup on a grocery store shelf. We were drawn together by a highly tuned sense of the ridiculous, which was probably one of the reasons why we enjoyed teaching middle school. We decided that we traveled well together and became even closer friends after a trip to Mexico.

Karen, the mother of three teenagers, had what Jane called a finely-honed bullshit detector. Jane, a four times married mother of none, could always make me laugh. She was a clever and creative teacher who once wrote a letter in a down-home Arkansas dialect to the Superintendent of the Petaluma City Schools, applying for a secretarial job, signing it "E. Z. Lei." Her criticism was usually easy to swallow because it was frosted with wit.

Several months after my divorce was final, my friends and I decided to take a trip to Los Angeles. Our first night in the hotel, after several glasses of wine, I began my rosary of resentments, spewing my dark, twisted Hail Marys of rage.

I related how we had met in high school and groped each other for several years in the front seat of his father's Oldsmobile. As a consequence, he was the first boy to touch my breasts. In my narrow Catholic enclave, that was reason enough to marry.

"He stole my maidenhood," I sobbed.

I remembered our younger days when Herb took a class where the participants took off their clothes and sketched each other in the nude. I told them how we smoked pot, which resulted in both of us dropping into deep slumber in the middle of many important philosophical discussions.

This reminded Jane of something I had told her about Herb. One night, when he was drinking heavily, he fell asleep when I was talking. When I shouted at him to open his eyes, he said, "If you were more interesting, I'd stay awake." Jane said that she sometimes had the same feeling as Herb after listening to me whine about the past. Although I was somewhat offended by her remark, I knew she was right.

Karen said, "Why can't you just bury the son of bitch? He's not coming back, so he might as well be dead."

"What if we have a mock funeral?" Jane suggested. "If we could symbolically bury him, maybe you could get on with your life."

I liked the idea. Remembering that Herb's cousin, George, was buried at Forest Lawn, I thought that if we could find the exact grave site, the ceremony would be more meaningful. George, a family icon, had died of leukemia at the age of twenty-four. He was a championship swimmer and an outstanding scholar. Until he had fallen ill, he'd had his own radio show broadcast from USC. Herb had grown up eclipsed by this handsome, gregarious cousin. Somehow, it seemed fitting that he be buried in the shadow of George's tomb. After several phone calls, we located the burial crypt in the Glendale branch of the cemetery.

The next step was constructing a symbolic corpse. Since Jane and I both smoked at the time, we pilfered a sugar bowl from a room service tray and half filled it with cigarette ashes. Rifling through our suitcases, we all found black clothing. Karen searched randomly through the Gideon Bible from the nightstand and came upon a passage that she thought was particularly appropriate. I gave life to a poem I'd conceived in my head some weeks ago. We had our ritual, and we were ready.

As we drove toward Glendale, I began to reminisce. "I always wanted Herb to be something different, more emotional, less even-tempered. It's interesting that the things I loved the most about him when we met were the things that I tried to change most after we were married awhile." I added, "I never saw him angry once, not even when he was drinking heavily."

There was a respectful silence.

Karen spoke up. "It sounds as if you were always looking behind him, trying to catch a glimpse of the person you wanted him to be. Now that he's dead, there's nothing left to change."

Forest Lawn at Glendale, in contrast to its namesake in Hollywood, was a modest memorial park. We saw no garish gravestones or enormous family crypts complete with stone benches and nightlights. There were many tombs marked by sorrowing angels, but none of them marked the graves of movie stars. When we finally reached the mausoleum that served as the final resting place for Herb's cousin, we found the corridor where he was buried closed off by a golden rope. Evidently, they were preparing for an interment the next day.

Boldly climbing over the barrier, we stood in front of the crypt. I was in the middle, with my two "angels" on either side. I lifted the sugar bowl full of "cremains" from a hotel laundry bag and placed it on the ground against the niche where George was buried. Karen's Bible passage, which contained the words "bitter herb," was most fitting.

Jane began her eulogy, "We are here to bury that son of a bitch, Herb Maloney . . ." It added an appropriately negative touch.

My poem, "Epitaph for a Marriage" was a catharsis for me.

The end of a marriage is worse than a death,
no wake, only a paper corpse of hopes and regrets.
"What if—If only I—If you had just—"
Your flesh exists.
It walks and breathes separate from me.
Oh, friend of my youth, green boy whom I loved,
You will never read this.

Afterwards, laughing hysterically, we saluted the marble angels and ran to our car.

*There comes a time when suddenly you realize
that laughter is something you remember
and that you were the one laughing.*

Marlene Dietrich

Ellen Sommers married several months after her nineteenth birthday and gave birth to six children before she turned thirty. When her youngest entered kindergarten, she entered the College of Marin, heeding her father's warning, "If you don't have an education and you need to work, all you can do is sell underwear at Macy's." She spent her career working with middle school students and loved every minute of it. Then Ellen "retired" and found herself in jail—first volunteering as a tutor at the County slammer and then teaching GED prep and whatever else she fancied. She finds jail fertile ground for a writer. She keeps a journal, and when she is old and gray, it might turn into a book.

In hindsight, what advice do you have for women going through a divorce?

First, scream for help. There are so many people out there going through the same thing. Get all the assistance you can to see you through the process—friends, church, if appropriate, therapy. Focus on work. Do some journal writing. Some of my best poetry was written then. Second, work hard to forgive if you were the wronged party. If you weren't the wronged party, work hard to forgive yourself for your part in the breakup. And third, don't get involved in another relationship until you've thoroughly worked out why the first one failed.

How do you get along with your ex today?
Although the kids were angry with him for a while and didn't want to spend holidays with him and his wife, we've all mellowed. We now spend Easter and Thanksgiving as a family. Herb and I have spoken on the phone and at family gatherings from time to time, but I am guarded in my conversations with him. He has become a very different person, and I find it hard to believe I was ever married to him. I've come to realize that we are both happier without each other.

Any new relationships since your divorce?
Right after my divorce, I had several disastrous dates. One was with a fifty-something gentleman who took me to a dance at a senior citizen's center which ended at nine o'clock. Another was with a man whom I met through a dating service—when I wondered why his nose was running, I discovered he was snorting cocaine in my bathroom. I also had a brief affair with a "professor" who worked for a diploma mill; however, when he admitted to being a Republican, the romance was over! I still date from time to time, but I've become addicted to the single life. Most men who are interested in me are too old. I can't envision myself spending my Golden Years feeding someone with a turkey baster in the old folks home.

Lost in Seattle

Sarah Franklin

Shivering in my urban-Londoner fashion parka, I gazed out beyond the ferry toward the San Juan Islands. In the Pacific Northwest, the landscape is everything. Its vastness flaunts your insignificance; you're literally at the brink of the earth. The sense of exile was too tangible to bear. I turned my face into the wind and wept.

Before this becomes a Victorian melodrama, I'll pause the pity party right here. Nobody had died. I hadn't maimed a royal corgi and been excommunicated from England. I was in the United States for the best of reasons, love and adventure.

I'd like to blame my husband for my misery, but honestly, it's all my fault. Three years ago, curled up in our North London condo with a notepad and a bottle of Cabernet, we'd made a wobbly list of pros and cons. Should we embrace Dave's transfer opportunity and move to Seattle? Dave, ever the techie, suggested writing a program to assign weight to the various considerations. I, the dreamer, waxed lyrical about snow-capped mountains, boat-fresh salmon, and our potential regrets if we didn't go while still young and foolhardy enough.

Ultimately, however, we decided "no." Sure, this was a fantastic opportunity, but so much tied us to England. I was sad to bid adventure farewell, but it made sense.

Three weeks later, I collected Dave at Heathrow Airport after a routine Seattle trip. Dave is one of those rare creatures who makes up his mind and then sticks to it. So I was unprepared for his first words as we negotiated the one-way system back onto the freeway toward our home.

"Let's move to Seattle! I've been thinking it through again, and it could be great."

"What, my angel?"

"Let's go! We can live outside the city, lakeside, with the quality of life we've been longing for. And you're right; if we don't try, we'll always wonder 'What if?'"

Like I said, he's the pragmatist, and I'm the idealist, so it didn't take much to convince me. "Let me think about it for a second—okay!" I agreed.

We were set on going, so we moved quickly. Our condo was rented, notices given, visas secured. Dave was borne through the myriad decisions by his deep-seated logic, and I was caught up in the romance. How often do you get to sail off into the great unknown these days? And the unknown it certainly was. Three business acquaintances aside, we knew not a soul in the Northwest, or much about the area itself beyond the *Fodor's Guide*. A mere five months later, we were waving goodbye to our former lives.

Then, like a balloon popping, the hectic stopped. We arrived in Seattle and into temporary company lodging. Focused on The Great Adventure, I'd ignored everything real about life overseas. I felt like Wylie Coyote: Having launched myself full tilt off the edge of a cliff, I looked around, legs pedaling furiously, only to discover a cavernous drop.

I hit the ground with a wallop on day two. Collecting me to meet our realtor for a day of house hunting, Dave discovered me crouching next to my suitcase, sobbing.

"Honey, what's up?" he asked, kneeling down to hug me.

"I can't," I sputtered.

"Sure you can! Just hang the sweaters up if the drawers are full. It's fine."

"Not that," I snuffled, outraged that Dave thought I'd disintegrate over a simple matter of closet etiquette. "I can't make myself unpack," I explained, blowing my nose on a sock.

"Okay, my sweet," said the ever-patient Dave. "Um . . . why not, exactly?"

"Because once I'm finished, I've got nothing left on my to-do list—ever!" I wailed. "I have no life. I'm nobody. And it's only just occurred to me. I know I'm slow, but I was swept up in visions of whale-watching and the scent of the cedars and sailing in the Sound at sunset. I forgot the living-an-everyday-life part. And you have your big, important job, and I have to snap out of it so that you can concentrate and not worry about your little wifey sitting at home with no friends and no plans and no hope. Oh, and no life."

For more than a week and a half, I slowly fell apart. Every morning, I'd discover that another scrap of my sense of self had eroded overnight. The losses piled up. My fantastic career. My monthly business trips within Europe. And, critically, my friends, each one as unique and necessary to me as every breath.

The innocuous question, "What do you do?" panicked me. So used to answering with the easy, "I'm in publishing," I was forsaken. What do I do? "I'm a corporate wife" was terrifying. Visions of Caesar salads and manicures flashed before me. Anyway, a true corporate wife required a chattering mass of cronies, and I'd left those behind, too. No more leisurely chats over a bottle of Cava. No more weekends teaching our five-year-old niece how to tease Dave. Sod the professional me; I'd lost the personal me, too. So who was I?

On top of my more existential panics, I had guilt. I was the girl with the golden ticket. I had met my soul mate. We were fulfilling a mutual ambition to see America for ourselves. Visa technicalities meant I couldn't work here for a full year. Ostensibly, I had the perfect scenario: unlimited time in the center of the universe with my husband and a ban on working.

My pal, Ann, had sighed one day at lunch in London. "You've got every person's dream. Total license to do whatever you want all year long."

So why did it feel less like a dream and more like a prison sentence? Increasingly, I was convinced I was broken. I couldn't relax into my good fortune.

When, two weeks on, my gloom hadn't lifted, Dave made a suggestion. "Temporary, corporate accommodation is depressing at the best of times," he said. "So why don't we go up to the islands at the weekend?"

And so here we were, the beauty filling me with sorrow, the mists in my mind rivaling the ones all around me.

Dave came up on deck. "This is no good," he said quietly as I huddled. "I'll let work know it's not going to pan out. We'll be home by Christmas. You can't stay this miserable. It's not fair."

I muttered something indistinguishable and curled up tighter to try to hide from the sadness. I'd wrecked everything. I'd blown the opportunity of a lifetime. My friends would think I lacked backbone, my parents would be softly disappointed that their great parenting hadn't made me a stronger person, and I'd be laughed at in the street: "Look! There's the loser who screwed up the best thing that could ever happen." And worse, I'd ruined things for Dave, whose gentleness made things unbearable. *I'm a total failure,* I thought.

And then my subconscious picked up on the word "failure," transmitting me a memory of a conversation in my favorite Soho restaurant four months previously. Discussing my Seattle move, my dear college friend Tom had asked what I'd do with my newfound spare time.

"Don't know," I'd shrugged.

"You can do anything you fancy. Why not have a stab at the portfolio arts lifestyle you've always fancied? Or learn Chinese; it'll sit nicely with your German major."

"Yeah, but what if I try this stuff I've always wanted to do and fail dismally?" I had asked.

"So what?" said Tom. "At least, you'll have tried. This isn't like the year you spent in Germany for your degree. There's no test at the end. You *can't* fail. You get the grades just for taking part in your own life."

I had muttered noncommittally and moved on to Tom's love life. And I'd entirely forgotten until my brain reconnected the word "failure" with this conversation.

I uncurled. Tom had been right. First, so what if I "fail"? And second, how could I, really? All I had to do was try to live my life the way it most made me happy.

I pulled off my hood. The fog was clearing. I turned to Dave. "Look! Isn't it beautiful?"

Dave pondered the rapidly approaching island, then me. "We're on dry land?"

"Yeah, I found some." I smiled for the first time since arriving. "I reckon I can try to make this work. How would that be?"

Needless to say, my long-suffering husband thought this would be just fine. Which isn't to say that life transformed into a Hallmark card. We had disassembled our London lives in super-speedy, road-running time, but building a new one is more like hiking. It's slow, it's painful, and half the time you're not positive you're even on the right track.

I learned to slow down and to cut myself some slack those days when simply buying groceries was a challenge. ("Zucchini? Where are the courgettes?" I'd puzzle.) After all, time I did have.

I discovered the great American tradition of volunteering through the Seattle International Film Festival. This helped me connect with our new hometown and also resulted in a friendship now one of my closest on any continent. I stopped trying to second-guess a year's worth of activities and imagined a day's worth. Then another day. Then a whole week. Then a month.

Dave and I spent many happy hours on our deck, enjoying Lake Washington and the extra time we had together now.

Of course, there were—are—still times when the flight to London calls me, when all I fancy is ten minutes talking to my sister, but it's four o'clock in the morning in England. But choosing to make this work is something I'll always be proud of. And crucially, I've gained confidence to just try anything and see what happens. After all, when it's your life, the only judge of success is you. So there is no such thing as "fail."

A ship in port is safe,
but that's not what ships are built for.

Grace Murray Hopper

Sarah Franklin was born and raised in the Forest of Dean, England and has lived in Austria and Germany. She studied Modern Languages at Cambridge University before moving to London to work with two loves of her life—travel and publishing. She currently lives with the third love of her life in a lakeside apartment just outside Seattle and has continued her career as a publishing professional and freelance writer. Eager to prove herself a true Northwesterner, Sarah has traded in her fondness for cute shoes for a mission to collect as many new pieces of

outdoor gear as her day jobs can support. What to actually do with them all, however, remains a mystery.

What else have you tried on a whim?

Nothing quite as drastic as moving countries, although I do tend to try and live by the "regret the things you do, not the things you don't do" motto, which can lead to fun. I recall one occasion at a railway station in Italy where I had an open ticket and decided to just to get on the next train and see where it took me. I wound up spending the most beautiful day in a tiny village in the Umbrian countryside, miles away from anywhere. It was definitely one of the highlights of the trip.

Have you been back to London?

Yes, several times. It's always wonderful to catch up with people again, but London itself just strikes us as impossibly hectic and unfriendly these days—or maybe we've just softened up!

Have friends and family come to visit?

We had a ton of visitors in our first year. The longest gap between guests all year was ten days. But things have calmed down a lot the longer we've been here. It's great to show people around, and because it's such an amazing place to live, they're guaranteed a fantastic vacation. It's fun to combine our two worlds.

What are some of the everyday differences between those two worlds?

It's a cliché, but people really are friendlier in the United States. Living among a positive vibe does wonders for giving you that feeling of being on vacation every day. On a very specific level, the huge access to the outdoors (on Sundays, we throw the kayaks in the lake and paddle up the shore for our coffee) makes life way more relaxing than fighting through public transportation for an hour. One thing I really miss, though, is the Sunday newspaper. Nothing beats the *Observer.*

Have you since obtained a work visa and a job?
Yes, I'm now the proud possessor of a United States working document and back in employment. Having a year away from the workplace gave me space to think about how I'd like my days to be, and I'm now really happy working three days a week at a wonderful publisher here in Seattle, while also freelancing for an arts organization and concentrating on my writing.

Our Day

❧

Elizabeth Eidlitz

My daughter, slouched in the back seat as I chauffeur her into New York City through heavy rain, is wearing sunglasses. Wires dangle from the headset clamped to her ears. She is unable to understand why, at fourteen, she can't borrow my credit card and shop with her friends. In breezy asides that make my emotional balance swing wildly, she's begun mentioning that she wants to live with her father.

Her ninth-grade advisor reassures me: This is a typical adolescent phase to be ignored; surely, I must remember how it was.

And I do. My memory of "Our Day," an idea my mother probably read in child-rearing manuals she trusted more than her heart, hasn't faded over the years. An uneasy parent, finally giving birth at thirty-nine after two miscarriages, perhaps she could not bring herself to love fully or spontaneously; too much had been taken away from her already.

One September Saturday when I was fourteen, I let the car's motion slide me over plastic seat covers, as mother, who always won at chess, crossed midtown Manhattan like the knight, catching green lights by angling down two blocks and over one. I had decided "Our Day" was her conscientious effort to try to like a child better by pretending closeness between us, hoping it might catch on.

"Wait here, sweetheart," she said, shifting into neutral to dump me at the Fifty-third Street parking lot by its No Vacancy sign while she sought the attendant. Translation: I might be snippy.

She'd never gotten over the time when a Canadian border customs inspector had asked, "Bringing anything special back to the States?" and I'd volunteered, "Only five sticks of dynamite," a nine-year-old's idea of funny. "Open that one," he'd pointed to a deeply buried bag. Wrestling with it, Mother had decapped a gallon of maple syrup that pulsed into the spare tire well.

In the parking lot, the attendant was massaging dollar bills into his jeans pocket while I kicked through gravel, hoping to scuff my tie shoes. Mother's heels clicked on pavement. I looked up into stabbing sunlight.

"Try not to do that with your face, darling. You'll get permanent frown lines."

Had I mentioned the No Vacancy sign, she'd have said, "Look, Elizabeth" (friends called me Liz), "obviously, there was room for another car." Nevertheless, an unspoken threat hung over our silence, like the sword suspended over that poor guy in Greek mythology. "I've planned Our Day—with lunch and theater after shopping, but if you have to ruin it . . . " would be one of her many unfinished sentences, like, "If you chew the ends of your glasses . . . if you don't stand up straight . . . if you loosen your retainer . . . if, at fourteen, you still haven't learned . . ."

A red light stopped me from walking behind her, imitating staccato steps behind her back. The green funneled us, side by side, into the crowd crossing Fifth Avenue. In Best & Company's elevator, I squeezed into the far corner. She shouldered closer to me to stage whisper, "Isn't it time for some grown-up underwear, too, Daughter?" Two ancient ladies were trying not to snicker.

In the Junior Miss viewing section on "Seventh Heaven," I slumped against couch cushions, arms locked across my chest, while mother told a saleslady, "We'd like to see some nice dresses. Daughter goes off to boarding school next week."

Then she'd be rid of me. Father divorced her five years earlier, sticking her with my "snippy and contrary" behavior. I considered placing myself for adoption with Bridge Over Troubled Waters; they help kids determined to work hard to overcome obstacles and improve their lives. I would work very hard.

I ran out of polite ways to say no to "smart little frocks" meant for May Queen types long before the saleswoman smiled and started toward the stockroom again for "just the thing."

Her first new offering was a West Point dress—one black vertical stripe dividing steel-gray flannel.

"No?" She stared disbelievingly.

Like a duck in a shooting gallery, the target fell over her arm. A blue one came up in its place. "Then how about this?"

She'd saved the best for last. The morning glory blue color startled me forward. The full skirt would waterfall over my knees. I'd toss two fringed lengths of material attached at the collar, scarf-like, over one shoulder. The three-quarter length sleeves would reveal my ID bracelet, engraved, "Love Always, Michael," a pretend gift I'd bought with my allowance after another summer at an all-girls camp.

"Like it, precious?" Mother's smile curled into poignancy. "Why not try it on?"

I heard it as an invitation to stand up straight so I didn't spoil the lines of the dress and turn slowly, giving her time to exchange winks with the saleslady about how I was "developing" before exclaiming, "How grown up you look!"

"We love it, don't we," Mother pleaded. "Rather try it on at home? It could be sent."

"Well, the color's nice. But—it's too sophist—"

"You needn't scowl, Elizabeth. No one's saying you have to have it."

On the rack, the dress was swinging in diminishing blue arcs. I longed to set it again in motion, but pleasing Mother would have raised her expectations, already too high for me.

I tried an extravagant sigh. "Have to have something. Let's buy that blue thing and get it over with."

"You'll never wear it if you don't like it, sweetheart. No point letting it hang in your closet."

I couldn't argue. In my closet, tags dangled from the Young Miss Bonwit's dress Mother had ordered months before from a *New Yorker* ad. And I couldn't utter the words "I love it."

"Sorry," Mother shrugged to the saleswoman. "Have to let it go, I'm afraid. No pleasing her today."

We marched uptown, tandem. "You have two choices," Mother announced, the back slash in her straight skirt moving like sharp scissors. "Pull yourself together for our nice day, or—if you have to ruin it—we'll forget the matinée and lunch at the Miyako and go straight home."

I think it would be nice to go straight home, I was tempted to lie. But west of Fifth Avenue, aromas of Japanese cooking crept into Fifty-sixth Street. "Up to you," I said. "I don't care."

Mother's arm locked mine, pressing it into her breast. "The smell's irresistible, Liz."

The food was beautiful. Artistic layers of razored, raw beef and necklaces of onion pearls simmered while we finished clear soup with tofu cubes and new moons of lemon peel.

"Oh!" Mother's glance zigzagged across rice bowls and plates. *"Boysan, aona ocha, kudasai."*

Bright-eyed, Boysan bobbed toward the kitchen for a pot of green tea.

The year before Father left, Mother took evening courses in Japanese flower arrangement and studied Japanese. Was it easier to communicate in a foreign language? I searched for something to say in the only one I knew, but merely bumped into the pressure to be interesting.

At the theater, Mother watched the orchestra seats fill. In whatever direction she turned, fused blues of her enamel pin sparkled. A fashion columnist might have written, "For 'Our Day,' Amanda Delamater (ex-Mrs. David S.), of this city and Canada, selected a wool checked suit. Displayed on a wide lapel was a pin. Her only child, Elizabeth, made it last year in copper enameling class."

I cuddled into my secret knowledge that Mother really, really liked it. Even loved it. I'd checked her jewelry case after she'd left for a weekend last spring and found only cotton inside the box. My expensive mother had chosen to wear my homemade pin, rather than her diamond brooch, even when I wouldn't be able to notice.

But what fashion editor could guess that the girl slouched in a soiled raincoat, pretending to read *Playbill*, twisting uncombed walnut hair while she prayed for the house lights to dim, belonged to the woman whose French braid made her look like the Dutchess of Kent in the royal box at Wimbledon?

After the curtain fell on magical transformations, we were forced together into the real world of late afternoon on Fifty-third Street. An older woman hailed my mother, a college classmate. I chewed a fingernail while they exchanged greetings.

"That's right, Ruth!" Mother exclaimed. "It's been thirty years."

"So this is your daughter." The stranger angled her head. "She doesn't look at all like you, Amanda, does she?"

"No," I announced. "I'm adopted."

Mother sputtered, "Oh, E-liz-abeth!"

Her friend seemed embarrassed.

My lie had divided them, leaving a thrilling dividend of doubt.

I stiffened for Mother's voice on the way to the parking lot, but didn't dare look at her. She reached into her purse for a hankie, paid the attendant, blew her nose.

In the car light that came on when she opened the driver's door, my pin looked tacky, out of place with her elegance, her savoir-faire. Though she'd desperately searched for something her daughter could do successfully, I kept letting her down.

Two years earlier, we'd argued about piano lessons. Stumbling on keys as I tried to sight-read, I'd wanted to stop.

"You get good only by practicing," Mother, who played by ear, insisted. "I'd hoped you would enjoy them. But I can never please you. You've rejected me since birth, refusing to breastfeed."

The silent return from "Our Day" was punctuated only by throat clearings, the metronome of windshield wipers, jangling coins for tolls.

I knew my most recent rejection of her, in front of her friend, was a terrible thing to have done. My mind kept practicing "I'm sorry." Yet my words, though true, never came out easily like hers.

I resolved to say them before the Seventy-ninth Street boat basin, but Mother drove too fast. Ninety-sixth Street then.

What if she died without knowing how sorry I was?

We passed Grant's Tomb.

The Cloisters.

Wasn't Mother's stony face proof enough that she didn't expect an apology? *Probably didn't even want it.*

I hunched into my raincoat while the rearview mirror shrank the span of the George Washington Bridge, whose lights outline connections across dark blue space.

Ten years later, teaching science at a school in Westchester and driving each week into the city after classes to see a therapist about compulsive overeating, I'd flip the rearview mirror to jettison the bridge view which evoked the pain of what might have been—a longed-for connection which, even at fourteen, I'd known I wanted.

Then, one April evening on my way out of the city, when I'd lost ten pounds, when my hair had been recently styled, when I was wearing the dress and heels I'd put on for a faculty luncheon, I stopped on impulse by the new apartment building where my mother lived alone, ready to offer unspoken words.

Street and bridge lights had come on, but her fifteenth-floor windows were dark. I parked across the street, waiting while the sky moved through sapphire blues. Her living room remained unlit.

A relief, actually. I could have been thinner, had a more prestigious job, called first, which mother preferred. She'd have wanted her lipstick on, her mind prepared for our talk, a devil's food cake in the refrigerator to please me.

The impulse never returned. With the ineluctable passage of days, it became too late for more than estrangement's unspoken truce, obligatory phone calls, and ritual exchanges of gifts probably neither of us particularly wanted. And I was busy. Besides, I'd met Steven and reluctantly agreed to quit my job for him.

Mother moved to Florida shortly after my wedding. I kept putting off dutiful visits. She died having seen only a snapshot of her baby granddaughter. At least, she never learned of my failed marriage after I returned to the satisfactions of teaching. Steven believed that falling in love meant losing oneself.

• • •

Another level has been added to the George Washington Bridge, and now I am the one in the driver's seat, unable to reach the daughter whose head nods to the beat of some "awesome" music.

"Where would you like to have lunch, Heather?" I had planned on a Japanese treat.

I have to ask twice before she removes the stereo earmuffs.

"I don't care. Just not oriental junk at that 'M' place you're always thrilling about."

"Miyako."

"Whatever."

"Ever eaten Japanese food?"

"Of course not!"

"Then why not try it?"

"Why would I try something I hate?"

My efforts to reach out, hoping to please her, backfire. I clench my teeth on the absurdity of her stunning logic, and frustration tightens my skin over muscles rigid as stone. *Thank goodness she's behind me and can't see my face.* Then I catch her hooded lenses in the rearview mirror.

She meets my mother's critical expression, sees the look which years ago I misread as stoic forbearance against the unacceptable daughter. What if Heather reads disdain, contempt, indifference in the reflection?

Instead of mourning lost opportunities to be the casual mom I yearned for, my sadness is for my mother, caught in that bind and bond of flesh and blood she could neither loosen nor heal. I recognize, too late, her shield against yearning. She would have thrilled to my unannounced visit. Yes, she would have told me that had I only called, she could have picked up a devil's food cake. Yes, she'd have fussed at the pins in her French roll. But her heart would have soared.

We pass Grant's Tomb.

How much time have Heather and I to waste?

I know better than to count on some accidental happy resolution of an adolescent phase. My own had not been just a stage I was going through. I managed to put its issues off until my thirties. Though I know how to confront friends without ruining friendships, confronting my daughter paralyzes me. When should I try harder? When should I walk away? She greets "How was school today?" with a hiccup of a sneer, and "Enjoy your weekend" with "Don't tell me what to do."

Are her responses so different from my prolonged aggressive defenses when the world felt unsafe, when I was afraid that letting things slide would make me appear weak, so I acted more powerful than I felt?

The paralysis my mother must have known is not the legacy I want for Heather. Or for grandchildren I dream of hugging in the flesh.

Panic readies me to turn off into the Seventy-ninth Street boat basin and into the parking area, even if a snippy voice says, "What are we stopping for?"

"I need to talk with you, darling. Now."

I'll expect her to fling her shoulders against the back seat, away from my urgency, while familiar words come forward: "Now what the hell have I done?"

"Nothing. Believe me." I'll struggle against tears which might seem manipulative. "Please come up front. It's important."

A lifeless pause may move in on my words, but I'll will these doors to open, watch rain drip off Medusa locks onto her Walkman. She'll remove her sunglasses, unmasking delft blue eyes, clear with challenge, but taking in mine.

"I want to tell you about 'Our Day.' No, please don't scowl. It's not this one. It was years ago, your grandmother's idea of a nice Mother-Daughter day of shopping, lunch, and theater. I was the daughter who could never measure up."

I'll steady myself, resting a tentative hand on her knee. More generous than I, Heather may allow tenderness that would have made me flinch.

It will open the way to confidences. I'll tell her about a beautiful, blue dress that I never tried on, even confess to the immediate thrill and long-term shame of emotionally disowning my mother in public.

Will my fiercely good intentions be filtered through mistrust? Heather could interpret my words as upstaging. Hear an implicit, *See? I was once more ornery and self-defeating than you could ever imagine being.* She'll put up with a burdensome monologue until she can take refuge in the back seat.

We stay on the highway.

For now, while silence stretches the invisible distance between us, my daughter and I are on our way into the city. Just a back-to-school shopping expedition, with a break for lunch. Yet, it's not 'Our Day' of only two options: pulling yourself together or going straight home. She needn't cast me as the East Coast Distributor for Guilt.

"About lunch, Heather. Your options are wide open."

"Papa Guido's?"

The question mark is her shield against anticipated objection.

"Papa Guido's, it is."

I remind myself that, in the process of becoming, she needs to belong, as I pay for low-rise jeans that reveal a fashionable amount of flesh and Heather spends her allowance on cosmetics that make her a clone of friends from buffoon city.

We slide over mended red plastic seats in a booth whose tabletop is smeared with swiped rag trails. Papa Guido himself, wiping his hands on a stained apron, takes our order. Our differences find easy compromise: her pizza half with little fishies, mushrooms on mine.

We are sharing layers of all the vital ingredients, and Heather is smiling as she uses a soggy triangle like a lacrosse stick to catch strings of melting mozzarella. We match each other with splats of tomato sauce that move us closer to a lifetime of authentic "Our Days."

❧

*People talk about "dysfunctional" families;
I've never seen any other kind.*

Sue Grafton

Elizabeth Eidlitz was born and raised in New York City. She now resides in Massachusetts, where she is a studio potter, teaches writing workshops and ceramics, and writes biweekly Sunday columns for a Boston-area newspaper, features for a local paper, and freelance articles for multiple magazines. Elizabeth writes at four o'clock in the morning, when she can watch the dawn and a squirrel who commutes from an oak tree, when UPS delivers nothing, the phone is silent, and the cat hasn't thrown up yet.

Did you try to change the way you related to your daughter after your epiphany about "Our Day"?

After that crash of insight, recognizing how Heather might misinterpret my expression just as I had misinterpreted my mother's and that she was acting out in ways analogous to how I behaved at her age, the way I saw her and so the way I related to her started to change. I became increasingly aware of how past relationships can insidiously affect present ones. When we have expectations about how our children are supposed to be, it can take them a long time to figure out, guilt free, who they really are. I'd always been at extremes with my daughter, alternating between being quite critical of her and hard on her, then letting her get away with some outrageous behavior. That's, of course, how my mother treated me. Can you imagine—never addressing my outrageous lie to her friend?

How has your relationship evolved over time?

We're still in transition as I move away from the edges. I used to be tremendously unforgiving of her. I've softened, in part, at least, from realizing that my mother was simply a flawed human being and not my enemy. I hope Heather has reached the same conclusion about me. Rather than keeping silent, I'm learning to speak my true feelings. Actually, everybody responds to that—friends, mothers, daughters alike.

Have you ever told Heather about your own "Our Days" with your mother?

That morning in the car, I stopped myself from laying the tale of "Our Day" on Heather. But she'll know about it now. Writing this story was telling her. She reads everything I write.

The Naked Date

Meera Lester

I was ready to nest when I first met Steve. He seemed different from most of the guys I attracted who pledged undying love with the goodnight kiss, then disappeared for a smoke and a twelve-hour romp with an old girlfriend. I didn't need a therapist to tell me that I had some major trust issues with men. But something about Steve told me maybe, just maybe, I could trust him.

He published a San Francisco Bay Area music magazine. I offered myself as free labor. I pressured Steve to make me a columnist, but he put me in sales. Hoping to please him, I said *yes* and gave it my all, even though I had never sold so much as a box of Girl Scout cookies. Attired in red spike heels and a short dress, I gulped down a double espresso before going out to meet storeowners who were total strangers and asking them to give me their money for empty space on a blank page. At the end of the day, I limped into Steve's office and delivered two

194

full pages of ads and an envelope full of checks. He hugged me, massaged my feet, and asked me out.

Now, the unwritten rules of a first date are pretty simple. You show up on time, dress appropriately, and don't talk about why your mother is in prison, why your last boyfriend left you for the bartender at the bowling alley, and why some of the women in your family have three breasts and six toes. I was really nervous, but just looking at Steve made my heart race. So I decided I'd go out with him, try to remember what *not* to do, and keep my radar tuned to detect signs of potential deception and betrayal.

Steve told me that we would be having dinner with one of his advertisers and, afterwards, we could do whatever we wanted. I promised to play my part as the perfect guest in order to get to the part where "we could do whatever we wanted." My mind raced with possibilities—a glass of chocolate port, a walk under the stars, jazz at a local club.

My immediate concern, however, was to not violate rule two—dress appropriately. Should I wear a summer suit or something more bohemian that expressed that wild side of me? Whatever I wore would have to go with sandals because of the blisters on my toes. I chose sexy low-rise jeans and a tank top, forgoing the underwear, which turned out to be an unfortunate decision.

When he picked me up for our date, Steve told me I had dressed perfectly for the occasion. The client lived in the woods, and the place was rustic. We began an animated conversation that continued right up to the point when we stopped in front of iron gates across the road. The letters announced Leapin'

Lodge. An old woman, buck naked, bent over and, looking like a shriveled prune in a floppy hat and worn sneakers, shuffled up to unlock the gate. We had arrived at a nudist camp.

I panicked. *No clothes. These people wear no clothes.* My mind flooded with images of being surrounded by naked strangers. And there was Steve, smiling as if this was the most normal thing in the world to do on a first date. How was I to eat and make conversation, keep my gaze focused on their eyes and not on their private parts, and perhaps linger over a cup of coffee and dessert, all the while trying to be poised, confident, and charming?

"These people have advertised with us for the last three years," Steve said. "It's an important account. Just relax. You'll be fine. This is my first time, too." I managed a feeble smile and tried to psyche myself.

We followed the woman up the hill to the camp café. I noticed pairs of men playing tennis, their fleshy appendages bouncing freely as they sprinted back and forth across the court. Oddly, they wore hats, socks, and shoes—nothing else, unless you counted sunscreen. Others in the buff relaxed in lawn chairs by the swimming pool. I felt conspicuously overdressed.

"You can change in there," the Prune said, pointing her finger toward the women's bathroom. How I wished I could change, all right—into a sombrero, a palm tree, just about anything other than my birthday suit.

I took my cue from Steve. He walked toward the men's room, so I followed the Prune to the toilet. I had two items to remove—jeans and a tank top. That would take less than a minute.

I pulled off my top and stared at my small breasts. *Uh, I don't think so, Miss Double-A-Cup Queen.* I put it back on. *Okay, this isn't working for me. I should just march right back out there and tell them—tell them what? That I was insecure about my body? Or that I was trying to impress my boss and it was a tad too soon to get naked?* A small but loud voice inside my head screamed: *Make a run for it. Never, under any circumstances, bare all to the man of your dreams on the first date under the harsh glare of kitchen lights with naked strangers watching. No man is worth that. No man, except maybe Steve. But what if he was just like all the other guys? He was the reason I found myself in this position. Hadn't he already deceived me? What made me think I could I trust him?*

The clink of glassware and animated chatter made me wonder how much time I'd spent in the john. Steve must have undressed and rejoined them. *They've started the meal without me.* I pulled my top off again and attempted to tie it into a bandanna around my chest, but the fabric wouldn't stretch. A button holding a strap popped off. I'd ruined the shirt. What did it matter? Everything would be in full view in a minute anyway.

I stopped fiddling with the top and began unfastening my five-button jeans. I looked down at my blindingly white legs with a hint of stubble and wished I'd had them waxed. As I recalled, other women at the table were different shades of nut-brown and were probably perfectly groomed. I mean, what self-respecting woman would come to dinner at a nudist camp and not shave her legs? I reminded myself to check this out. Then it occurred to me that maybe the whole dress-for-success thing was overrated. After all, Steve's opinion about me had little to do with my clothes. And on the plus side, I'd get to see him naked, too. *Oh, hello.* Now I was curious.

After a half-hour of doing Lucy Ricardo in front of the mirror, I finally mustered enough nerve to make my way to the table. All eyes were on me. Okay, another rule: *Never make a late entrance when you're dining naked.*

The two legs of my jeans hung like sweater arms over my shoulders. The denim fabric concealed my breasts. But there was still the other problem below. By strategically clutching my tank top in a ball just below my belly button, I believed I successfully blocked that view, as well. I must have looked ridiculous strolling across the room and awkwardly slipping into the seat next to Steve. He looked pretty darn good shirtless, although I didn't look too far below the nipple line. I mean, this was our first date.

Steve smiled awkwardly as if sorry he'd gotten me into this. He gave my hand a supportive squeeze.

Okay, bring on the food. I wanted to gulp down the meal, get the docs signed, put my clothes back on, and hit the road. But the host, a large, burly man with nothing but a suntan accentuating his lackluster features, poured me a glass of ice tea and began chatting about how many new members had joined since he began advertising in the magazine.

His wife eventually emerged from the kitchen with bowls of cold vichyssoise on a tray. She wore an apron, and her large pendulous breasts were splotchy and stretched out like pizza dough. *Don't stare; it's not polite,* my mother's words intruded from the past. I kept my eyes on my bowl as the woman lifted it from the tray.

I'm sure I saw something slip in, then out, of the bowl. I looked at Steve to see if he'd noticed, but he was grinning at me as if I was the most beautiful girl in the world. I let the moment pass. What could I have said anyway that would have been polite? *Excuse me. Your breast grazed my soup. Would you please get me another bowl?* I don't think so.

Several of the guests were engaged in conversation. Steve leaned over and asked me if I'd like to listen to a new band with him later on after dinner. I asked him if we could leave right then. He shook his head and kept asking me questions. He wanted to know everything about me. So absorbed was I in the conversation between us that followed, I completely forgot we were naked. By the time the salad was served, we were just two people connecting our hearts through the thread of conversation. I don't know exactly when I no longer felt like a fish out of water, but sometime between the salad and main course, I began to trust Steve. And not only him, but everyone present. I pushed the jeans off my shoulders, and they fell to the floor. No one gasped or snickered or even looked over at me. Steve, however, in what I took to be a sign of approval, wiggled his brows up and down Groucho-style.

Then the dessert came and went. And just when I thought the whole ordeal was over—that we'd put on our clothes and go—the other shoe dropped.

"Join us for a walk in the woods, maybe a swim in the European pool up the hill a ways. We're certainly dressed for a swim," the big, burly fellow chuckled. I wanted to punch him, but smiled sweetly and suggested that it was probably getting a little chilly out now. "That's what the walk is for," he replied, grinning like a Cheshire cat. "You'll be ready for a swim when we get to the top."

Gritting my teeth, I huffed and puffed behind a line of nude men. The women stayed to do the dishes. Steve walked beside me, holding my hand. "I like your spunk," he said.

"You could have given me a heads-up," I said.

"I'm sorry," he answered. "It's just that I was afraid you might say no, and I wanted to be with you. Anyway, you passed my test. I can tell we're going to be good together, good for each other."

We had reached the top of the hill, and one by one, the men leapt into the pool.

I put my hand on Steve's arm. "Good for each other? Are you sure? You can know something like that already?"

"Yes." He pulled me aside and kissed me, then jumped into the cold water. I sat on the edge, waiting for him to swim over and climb out.

"Hypothetically," I asked, as he dripped dry next to me, "if you and I were to get something going, you wouldn't one day go out for a smoke and never come back, would you?"

He smiled. "And leave you? Not on your life. Besides, I don't smoke."

My heart pounded. In that vulnerable moment when my heart was as exposed as the rest of me, I felt curiously safe and certain that I could trust him with my life.

*Whatever our souls are made of,
his and mine are the same.*

Emily Brontë

Meera Lester is an internationally published author based in San Jose, California. She has written and had published four non-fiction books in the last three years. An avid oil painter, Meera painted the cover image and thirty-six portraits of saints in her recent book, Saints' Blessings: Wisdom and Guidance Inspired by the World's Most Beloved Saints. *She served as editor to several publications throughout her career and directed the Selling to Hollywood screenwriting conference for twelve years.*

Have to ask: Do any of the women in your family actually have three breasts and six toes?
Nah, our family flaws aren't so obvious. But I've inherited a wicked sense of humor and a love of practical jokes that sometimes gets me into trouble.

Was Steve "the one" for you?
Absolutely. I couldn't have asked for a more perfect man for me. We knew within three weeks after that first date that we always wanted to be together. He took me to San Francisco's Japanese Tea Garden where we walked to a small bridge that

arched over the water. He knelt and placed a ring on my finger, promising never to abandon me.

Are you still together today?

No, sadly, fate intervened. We built a lovely little nest, had a son, and remained married for twenty years. We'd still be married if it weren't for Steve's having to undergo a heart transplant at age forty-six. He died from complications eight months later. It's been three years now since he passed away, and sometimes I still think I'll turn around and find him standing at the ready, anticipating our next big adventure, his eyes twinkling and his boyish smile concealing some devious little plot. I'm learning to live with the emptiness that comes with loss. But remembering our first date at the nudist camp never fails to bring a smile to my lips.

Sleep, Sanity, and the Silver Bomber

Kimberly Chisholm

"So," he says. And I laugh. My mother's psychiatrist sits on his big squashy couch across from the smaller squashy armchair I've chosen.

"So," I say it this time and laugh some more. This laughter feels good, honest, and real. I'm sure that my mom, who has been seeing this man for a decade, has told Russell all about why I've come. I like and trust him immediately.

"You probably want my version of why I'm here."

"Sure." Russell is a big man, handsome with cropped gray hair, a perfect cross between Hemingway and my wise dissertation advisor. I tuck a foot under me and settle in.

"Okay," I say. "So." Fifty minutes stretch before me— none of my three kids tugging at my sleeve, no dishwasher to unload, no carpools to run—nearly an hour of self-indulgent introspection.

"Here's the thing," I say. "Everything is really good. I've got an IUD, the kids are manageable—well, mostly—and even though Bill travels a lot, things with him are so great."

"That sounds good." Russell smiles.

"Yes! After seven years of being pregnant or full-time lactating, I feel like I'm starting to have my life back."

"And that feels good."

"So good. I bound out of bed every morning at five to write before the kids are up."

"That sounds great," he says.

"It is. But . . ."

The corners of Russell's mouth turn down.

I furrow my brow.

"There are these nights." My voice holds steady only because I'm not in the infuriating, desperate midst of it. "I'll be going through these little bedtime routines that are supposed to soothe the kids—reading stories or singing songs or kissing a zillion baby dolls goodnight—and this awful dread starts building in me. All three kids have been horrible sleepers. All I can think about is how I won't be asleep for hours and it will be so hard to wake up the next morning to write. I just about die without my morning hours."

"Mmmm." Russell nods.

"It'll be after nine, and they're all wide awake. So I cave. It's gotten so I end up lying in Andie's twin bed, all hot and uncomfortable, but I lie there super still even though I'm seething inside, just hoping that they'll fall asleep. And of course, they don't. Quentin's plastered to my front; he's still nursing all night. And Andie's pressed against my back, doing this awful thing where she fiddles with my earring, whining it's the only way she'll ever fall sleep."

"And you feel . . . trapped?"

"Yes! And it gets worse. Andie so knows how to get a rise out of me. She sits up little by little with this crafty grin I can feel even in the dark. Or she keeps sliding her feet around or tapping her toes against me. And right now, she's obsessed—I'm told it's normal in a four-year-old, but it's really creepy—with death. I'm lying there all rigid, and she'll say, 'Mommy? What's the difference between dying and getting killed?' Not something I want to explore right before bed. Then in this horrible sing-songy voice she'll say: 'Mom-my . . . I'm not ti-red . . .'"

My imitation in Russell's office shuttles me back to the night before. In the dark heat of tangled blankets, my daughter's hot little face is right there in my ear: "Mom-my . . . I'm not ti-red . . ." I want to love her bright strength, but her needling cadence infuriates. I sit. I swivel toward her. Andie actually cringes. I have to pull Quentin to me because the poor baby is scared of what might come next.

And I am mortified—this is not the mother I am.

I suppress the screaming that threatens my every fiber. I jangle. I smolder. I want to hurl my daughter across the room. She has pushed me far enough again this night that I won't fall asleep for hours, even if she were to nod off this very moment. But it will be midnight before any of us sleeps. I won't get to write the next morning. The day will be horrific.

I rip off the comforter and stalk out of her room, Quentin on my hip. I slam the door. I hear her scrambling out of bed and across the hardwood floor. She throws herself at the door that

I have been advised not to lock, but whose knob I pull against, holding it shut.

And some nights I do scream. I get close in her narrow little bed and scream:

"WHAT AM I SUPPOSED TO DO WITH YOU?"

I scream so loudly that Quentin cries, and then I cry because this is not how I mother. I am not a mother who threatens and screams and grabs her daughter by the shoulders so tightly she has to check to be sure she didn't bruise her.

Yet bedtime goes on and on. Time-outs double and treble. I cave. And I cave further and let Andie into my bed where she insists on more earring fiddling, and I cannot stand it. I drag her back to her room. I sit on the floor just outside her door, and poor Quentin falls asleep in my arms, and poor six-year-old Will comes to his doorway, checking to be sure everything's okay. It's ten. It approaches eleven, and still she maintains her monologue from her bed, still she sneaks to her forbidden doorway, still that needling, sing-songy, "Mom-my . . . I'm not ti-red." My morning hours evaporate. And most nights Quentin cries, some nights I cry and sometimes I scream, and every once in a long while, Andie cries, too. So my mom, a psychiatrist herself, suggests I go to see Russell. Our family's proclivity toward depression and anxiety, coupled with her solid faith in the efficacy of short-term medication, lead her to believe I might benefit from a quick visit.

"Psychopharmacology is amazing stuff," I agree, "but I'm not anxious or depressed," which she, my closest confidante, already knows.

Eleven-thirty, though, in the eye of the next bedtime maelstrom, I sit fuming and teary in the hallway outside Andie's room. Quentin in my arms, telephone at my ear, I tell my mom, "Maybe I will call Russell."

"Bedtime sounds really," he shifts on his squashy couch, "hard."

"Yeah. It's awful."

"So," he says. I chuckle at how our little refrain under-scores how neatly this fifty minutes promises to solve my prob-lem. "Firstly, you don't sound depressed. You sound good."

I nod.

"It just seems like you could use a little . . . patience."

"Yes."

"Here's one idea. You could take a very low dose of any number of antidepressants. More and more frequently, a small dose—a quarter of the usual recommendation—is being pre-scribed to . . . buy a little patience. I wouldn't expect you to notice any changes, just that when you lie there, feeling trapped and afraid of losing control," Russell waits for me to acknowl-edge that this isn't overstatement, "we might just take that edge off."

I grin. "Sounds good."

"There are some side effects."

This isn't worrisome; this is the list he has to deliver by law. "Like?"

"Nothing serious. Loss of appetite, lethargy, sexual dys-function. But with such a small dose, I'd be surprised to see any of that."

"So," again I chuckle at our refrain, "out of curiosity, what exactly does sexual dysfunction mean? Our sex life is kind of important to me."

"Sure. Well, there's the obvious: decreased desire. But sexual dysfunction can also manifest itself in the sense that you are about to have an orgasm, but it's difficult to achieve. Though again, that's highly unlikely at this dosage."

It was exactly as Russell promised. Bedtime would roll around and the earring fiddling wasn't annoying. I didn't feel hot or trapped. Andie would ask "How do you know you're dying?" and I would reel off some fanciful, reassuring answer. Already, Quentin would have drifted off beside me, and—because I wasn't smoldering and ready to unleash who-knew-what, because I was a woman who had figured out one important way to take care of herself—Andie also would sleep.

Yes, bedtime improved dramatically, but it still meant Bill nodding off mid-story in Will's room and small bodies sprawled in the matrimonial bed. Bedtime almost never meant sex.

Instead, Bill and I stole time in the afternoons.

Three P.M. on a Saturday a few weeks after I meet with Russell, Bill is setting the kids up with the current Tivo favorite. He sprints upstairs and locks the door where I await in slinky lingerie, the vibrator extracted from the sock drawer. The silver bomber has become a necessity given that Bill and I have about twelve minutes before one of the kids realizes that something interesting may be transpiring in such an unusually quiet house. Eight minutes go by, and ten, and even with the trusty silver bomber, it's not looking good for me. Bill does his thing—just as the pounding begins on the door, Andie yelling, "Open up! I can break this thing down, you know!"

With a sympathetic kiss, Bill leaves me to my devices.

When I descend fifteen minutes later, he looks up from a gigantic floor puzzle. "Get it done?"

"Yeah," I say. "But touch and go." Then, with a little wonder, "I think this might be the dysfunction."

A few evenings later, Bill arranges the kids in a postprandial art project. "You go get a head start," he says. "The dysfunction and all."

Another day, in the market, I brandish the latest Disney DVD and say to him, "Maybe we need this. For the dysfunction."

I talk to my mom. "It's surprising," she says, "with such a small dose. But most side effects go away after a few months."

I talk to my sister, the nurse practitioner. "That's weird. Five milligrams? Weird." Then, because she's younger and doesn't have kids yet, she says, "Maybe get a baby-sitter and take your time."

The following Sunday morning, we're only a few minutes into it, but very little is going on and I'm getting tired of the whole thing—and it hits me.

"Wait," I say to Bill. I zip downstairs naked, not a single head turning from the elaborate fort the kids have been commissioned to build.

In any other household, I might be standing in front of the junk drawer, but ours is the "utility" drawer. I myself transformed it with these cool organizers that separate the various screwdrivers from the spare keys from the battery-powered emergency radio from the extra fuses. Granted, enough stuff gets stashed here that it's difficult to see the organizers, but the point is, they're there. What's important is that I am a woman who can wield a screwdriver and change out a fuse when pressed. I am a woman who dealt a serious blow to gnarly bedtimes and who knows the exact location of what she needs—there in the rear section of the utility drawer.

Back upstairs, I straddle Bill, grinning, one hand behind my back, the silver bomber in the other.

Triumphantly, I whip out two C-size batteries. "Say good-bye to what was never dysfunction! That was just a sad pair of overused batteries!"

I deftly change them, reveling in the eight minutes left to us. Eight prized minutes, all made possible by some sage advice, some solid support, and the desire to fix a thing or two.

*Home is a place not only of strong affections,
but of entire unreserve; it is life's undress rehearsal,
its backroom, its dressing room.*

Harriet Beecher Stowe

Kimberly Chisholm lives near San Francisco with her husband and children, who, now at three, five, and seven, are just beginning to sleep through the night. Kimberly is currently getting up at four o'clock each morning, instead of her usual five, because she is hot and heavy at work polishing a novel depicting— among other juicy things—the life of her great-grandfather, the

sculptor of Mt. Rushmore. After getting her Ph.D. in Spanish and French Literature at UC Berkeley in 2001, Kimberly started to write fiction both to save her sanity and to capture some of the intensely rewarding moments her children offered up even as they mired her in Play-doh and diapers and endless hours at the park. In her free time (ha!), Kimberly squirrels herself away with a book and hopes her children won't come looking for her. She teaches the occasional literature course at Berkeley and has published stories in Moxie, Bellowing Ark, Spindrift, *and online at* Literary Mama.

So, how's bedtime these days?

It's amazing. After seven years of completely shitty sleep, we are all finally making it through the night. Here's the secret: all five of us in one room. First, we dragged in a crib mattress. A few nights later, the trundle-bed mattress. Finally, the little cheap-o Dora the Explorer foldout couch. Bedtime rolls around, and we all climb into our respective beds (with our respective books on especially good nights!) and ten minutes later, everyone's out. Clearly, this approach wouldn't work for all families and might not have evolved this way if Bill didn't travel so much, but both he and I love it—like a nightly slumber party or a summer camp cabin.

Do you and Bill get more than twelve minutes now?

Maybe twenty. At a recent erotic dance class, a mom of older kids revealed that she and her husband have always simply said: "Mommy and Daddy are going to have some alone time." I wasn't sure Bill would go for this, but—not so surprisingly—he embraced it fully. It's the best. Very liberating and honest and has really cut down on the kids' suspicion (even Andie's, which is the key to the extra eight minutes).

What's the story behind the silver bomber?

Bill got it for me at some point soon after our first child was born. Maybe he sensed the time pressure and intuitively knew how to solve the problem? Since then, I've been giving vibrators to friends at every opportunity. For me, every "New Mommy Basket" feels incomplete without one.

I offer these three tips to the moms: Don't laugh too hard when you are innocently hanging out with your spouse and your three-year-old wanders into the room, scared out of her mind because the bottom drawer of the armoire really does sound like it's full of terrible rumbly monsters.

Don't be afraid to travel with your vibrator. Although vibrating suitcases are apparently far more suspicious to airline security personnel than ticking ones, avoid this by removing the battery before you go. Also, carry-ons are far less of a problem than you'd think. On the two occasions where a big, burly security guard rummaged through my bag, neither even lifted an eyebrow when coming across the old bomber buried at the bottom. One guy did hold up the device rather conspicuously while he worked, and quite a few people noticed, but everyone was thoroughly nonplussed, which I loved—imagining that dozens of vibrators come through those lines every day.

Lastly, when staying in swanky hotels, remember the housekeeping people pop in to turn down the sheets and tidy up in the evening, or you—like me—might find your favorite accoutrement lined up on its end right next to your toothbrush, lipstick, and mascara on that cute towel they put down by the bathroom sink.

What will your mother-in-law think when she reads this story?

My poor mother-in-law. (Poor Bill for that matter. Good thing he is so incredibly comfortable with all this.) My in-laws are from Boston. They are conservative Republicans, not big into breastfeeding or our current sleeping arrangement or my fanaticism about organic dairy products. But the thing is—and I love reminding Bill of this—his mother is a very sensual woman. She is beautiful and curvaceous in a lot of places I'm not, and men love her. The woman also, get this, went in for her six-week postpartum appointment after Bill was born and was pregnant. She had two non-twin babies in one calendar year. So, though I'm not wild about chatting up the Prozac, which is stupid as it should carry no stigma, I think she'll appreciate the sex part. I can't say, though, that I'm racing out to buy her a silver bomber of her own.

The Back Road to Enlightenment

Lauren Cassel Brownell

I missed my flight. Subconsciously, I'd probably wanted to miss it. I had to be in Corpus Christi by 8:00 A.M. to conduct a training seminar. Glancing at my watch, I dragged my bag over to the Avis rental counter in the deserted Lafayette terminal. It was six-thirty. I would have to drive all night.

I stepped out of the airport into a hot Louisiana summer's eve and hit the road. I usually enjoy the solitude of driving and can find beauty or at least something interesting to look at in my surroundings, but that evening was different. I found no serenity. Only reminders of the decisions I needed to make. I had met and fallen in love with a wonderful man, and we wanted to set a date for our wedding. I wanted a home and a family. And every click of the odometer was taking me farther from home. Every side road seemed like a symbolic alternative path I could choose.

For several years, I'd flown all over the country, several trips a month, to pursue my career as a corporate sales trainer.

I loved the job and the people I worked with. But I started to realize there was more to life than work. I wanted a job that didn't find me waking up at a La Quinta at three o'clock in the morning, not knowing where I was. The glamour was wearing thin. And yet, I was making an incredible amount of money. I was working for a company that I had helped create and desperately wanted to see succeed.

My mind flooded with questions: Did I want to continue to do this kind of work? Did I want to go to graduate school? Was I ready to marry?

I was at a crossroads.

I had gone as far as the interstate would take me on my journey. After making it around Houston, I checked the map to find the exit to the state road to Corpus.

I could hardly keep my eyes open. A cup of coffee was top priority. But the small two-lane road on which I found myself—heading away from the bright lights and big city of Houston and deep into the Texas countryside—did not appear to be a Starbucks-rich environment.

The next place I see, I'll stop and stretch and get something to drink, I thought to myself. I turned on the radio for company and sang along to a few classic rock tunes. Three songs became six, and then the DJ's voice broke through the music and said, "You've just completed a ten-in-a-row Rock Block with K-R-O-K." I had been driving for over half an hour with no signs of life.

After an eternity, my high beams reflected off a lone billboard on the side of the road. Billboard is too strong a word. It was an old road sign with the paint wearing off. The words were barely visible. As I got closer, I could just make it out:

Tired? Hungry? Budda's Café
Open 24 hours a day
Two miles ahead

My initial response was relief at the thought of an impending break. Then I started to laugh. *Budda's Café? Somebody out here has a sense of humor.* Way down a country road in rural Texas, someone was "new agey" enough to have named their place Buddha's, but lacked the savvy to spell it right.

One mile ticked off the odometer. *One to go.* In the distance, I saw a small, low building. It looked completely deserted—no people, no cars. As I drew up in front, I saw a neon "open" sign blinking on and off in the window. I put my rental car in park and turned off the engine. *Please be open. Please be open,* I prayed.

The door pushed open, and a wave of cool air-conditioned air hit me. I felt better immediately. There were five tables inside, each covered with a red-and-white checkered tablecloth with the obligatory salt, pepper, and ketchup. An older woman was sitting at one of the tables. A cigarette burned in the ashtray to her right. Her hands deftly twirled a fork and a knife together in a white paper napkin, and she added it to the stack on her left. She nodded in my direction but never stopped her systematic twist, fold, place of the silverware.

A girl of about fifteen sat at the counter that ran along the back wall of the restaurant. She had an apron tied around her waist and in its pocket was tucked a notepad and a pen. *The waitress,* I gathered. But at midnight, in the middle of nowhere, there was no one to wait on. I was the only customer at Budda's Café.

Through the short-order window that led to the kitchen, I could see a small old man with white tufts of hair on each side of his head. He peered out at me.

"What would you like?" he asked, coming out from the kitchen.

"I'd just like a cup of coffee," I said.

He was silent, tilted his head to one side, and looked at me. His hand went up to his chin, and he rubbed it thoughtfully.

Finally, he said, "Everything you need is right there." He pointed past me.

I turned and looked. A pot full of steaming coffee sat on a corner table that I hadn't noticed when I first walked in. Creamer, sugar, and spoons were all laid out neatly alongside. Cups were stacked nearby. Propped up against the wall was a sign made out of cardboard. In neat, block letters, it read: "Help yourself."

I looked back at the old man. He nodded.

I went to the table and poured myself a cup. I sat back down and sipped it, enjoying the silence as the three employees of Budda's Café went about their business.

I knew then exactly what to do. I had known all along. It just took an overnight drive, exhaustion, and a well-named roadside diner to help me see.

"What do I owe you?" I asked the proprietor when I was finished.

"This one's on the house."

I stepped outside into the heart of the Texas night. It was cooler than when I had gone inside. There was no moon, but millions of stars twinkled in the black sky and a gentle breeze was blowing. I glanced back at the sign above the door.

"Bubba's Café," it read. Clearly.

Bubba. Of course. Where had I gotten Budda? Had it just been a figment of my imagination? Had it been a cosmic message meant just for me? Or perhaps, at that moment, I'd been open to the universe and simply paying attention to the signs. Then I realized I was trying too hard to make it make sense. Buddha, Budda, or Bubba—it didn't matter. The wisdom was the same.

Everything you need is right there. Help yourself.

With caffeine and a newfound calm coursing through my veins, I made it to my destination with time to spare and delivered my most inspired training session. I managed to make the return flight home that evening, called my boss as soon as I walked in the door, and tendered my resignation. I've never regretted the decision—not for a single second.

There is something about the unexpected that moves us.
As if the whole of existence is paid for in some way,
except for that one moment, which is free.

Rose Tremain

Lauren Cassel Brownell lives with her husband and three children in Abilene, Texas. She has lived and worked all over the

country and has found great diners down country roads every-
where she's traveled. Her work has appeared in the anthology
Cup of Comfort for Women *(Adams Media, 2002), magazines*
such as Baton Rouge Parents *and* Purple & Gold, *and numerous*
community newspapers in suburban Philadelphia. She has con-
tinued her work as a writer, trainer, and motivational speaker
and is presently an advertising manager at the Reporter-News
in Abilene, Texas.

Once you handed in your resignation, what did you do next?

What became so clear to me that night was how much I loved
the man who would become my husband. Anything that kept
me away from him for an extended period of time was not
worth it, and anything I could do in life was meaningless without him. So I took some time off and planned our wedding. We
married three months later in a cozy ceremony with our closest
friends and family, and we're happily married today with three
children, one from his previous marriage. No journey has ever
been more life-changing or fulfilling than being married to the
love of my life and raising our family.

Did you eventually find a job that struck a balance for you?

I found balance on a personal level, but am still trying to find
that balance professionally. I'm a classic example of not knowing what I want to be when I grow up. I have been a mall marketing director. A marketing consultant. A stay-at-home mom.
An entrepreneur. All have had their good qualities and their

bad. When I was at home, I was bored and unfulfilled. When I was at work, I missed my children desperately. Now that the children are a little bit older, I have returned to a challenging and rewarding position in an organization that values the importance of families. So I'm optimistic that I may have finally found that balance for which I've been searching.

How do you keep yourself from going overboard in your work life now?

That's easy. My family always comes first. There's absolutely no question about that. It helps me set my priorities. But I give my very best at work when I'm there, and I give my very best to my family when I'm home. And I sleep like a baby every night!

Have you ever been back to Bubba's?

I've never even wanted to go back to Bubba's. I'm afraid that if I ever saw it in the light of day, it would ruin the magic and mystery of that night. It's like hallowed ground in my mind. I go back and visit in my imagination, and I do wonder what has become of Bubba's employees. But no, I've never been back, and I plan to keep it that way. I've found that sometimes it's best to just let things be.

Sixteen

Michaela Galley

I watch the beautiful young man through a gap in the frosted glass that divides the rows of booths in Carl's Jr. My four-year-old daughter twists around and smiles at him, flirting.

"Sit down on your bottom, Sarah," I say for the third time, gently pulling her to a seated position. "Finish your lunch."

I glance up, but the boy hasn't noticed us. He's deeply engrossed in a book. No older than twenty, he has a scruffy beard and wears a knit cap. He gets up to refill his cup from the soda machine. When he passes, I notice my bare left hand—I'd forgotten to put on my ring after my workout. I am sixteen again. I flash a smile. I am invisible to him.

I take a bite of my chicken sandwich that is too large and cover my mouth with a napkin while I contend with chewing. A middle-aged postal worker, seated alone with a newspaper, watches me with interest. I am thirty-five now, a wife, a mother. What if I could find her again, the sixteen-year-old? Could she and I meet and coexist? That night, before sleep finds me, I try to resurrect her.

My sophomore year in high school, I'm dating Seth, my first serious boyfriend. Seth and I meet at a steakhouse restaurant where we both work. He's a cook. I work on the salad bar. It's an awful job. I spend most of my time in a freezing-cold walk-in refrigerator, wrestling with vegetables and salad dressing to replenish the all-you-can-eat trough. The best part of the day is when I roll place settings in the back and flirt with the cooks. Most of them are young surfers, guys who love working nights so they can surf all day. Seth is by far the cutest, but he's shy. He's eighteen and has already graduated from high school. He shares a small apartment with a roommate and works full time.

At first, I try to discreetly take my breaks when he does. We talk while I drink soda and he smokes Marlboro Reds. He always apologizes for his smoking and insists that he's trying to quit. I don't care; I have a huge crush on him. He drives a green VW Beetle with surf racks.

I'm surprised when Seth asks me out for the first time. I never thought I was in his league. It's a real date. He picks me up at my house, he takes me for lunch at a restaurant on the waterfront, and we eat fried calamari and talk. On our next date, we have dinner at a Mexican restaurant. Afterwards, we drive down to the beach to watch the surf and sunset. Seth asks if it's okay to kiss me. I appreciate his politeness, but I'm so nervous, I'm shaking. I hate my braces and explain that it might be kind of a drag, me wearing braces and all. He says he doesn't mind and asks again if he can kiss me.

"Sure," I say, and he leans in.

It's so nice. Even with braces and despite my anxiety. Seth acts as if he's lucky to have me. When he kisses me that first time, I can literally feel his appreciation, his gratitude for being able to touch me. His words make me feel like the most beautiful girl in the world. It's intoxicating to have this power over someone whom I welcome touching me. He is tender and honest and, in many ways, innocent.

As the memory of Seth and our first kiss recedes, I turn over to watch my sleeping husband, Steve. I try to recall *our* first kiss.

We're in college and dating other people. Steve and I gradually become best friends, and our respective relationships end. We're drunk one night, and an equally inebriated mutual acquaintance suggests that the two of us "try kissing to see if there are any sparks." We oblige, and it's awkward at first, but it leaves me wanting more. We bypass traditional courtship and move in together.

●   ●   ●

It's a week after my fast-food epiphany, and I'm sitting at my computer, waiting and perspiring. Only nine minutes left. I call Steve at work.

"I think we got it," I say. "There haven't been any new bids for an hour."

"How much longer?"

"Nine minutes. This is so stressful. How do people do this? I'll never buy anything this way again. I can't take it."

"Go into the living room and listen to Incubus, *Aqueous Transmission*. It's at least four minutes. You'll relax."

"Good idea. I'll call you when it's over."

I start the CD, take a few deep breaths, and try to relax. When the song ends, I go to the computer to check the auction. Another bid came in. Four minutes left. The current bid exceeds the amount Steve and I agreed to the night before. I have to decide. There's no time to call him. I am sixteen again. I type in a new bid, $500 more, as high as I'll go. I hit "enter" and walk away.

I replay the song. When it ends, I check the computer. I've won. I'm exhilarated and nervous at the same time. I call my husband and tell him the good news. He's not upset over the extra cost.

We'd stayed up until 1:00 A.M. the night before. I'd tried to introduce him to her, the girl who is sixteen. I'd kept her hidden all these years.

"Imagine I'm a complete stranger," I said. "You've never met me, and you want to know me. You want to date me; you want to get me into bed. How will you achieve your goal?"

My husband laughed, his forehead crinkled. "Good question," he said.

"I'm serious. The girl inside me needs to be courted, romanced—seduced. I can't keep stuffing that part down. You're my best friend, you're my partner and a wonderful father, but I know there's a passionate person inside. I know you have it in you," I said, and I kissed him softly.

"Okay," he answered. "This could actually be fun."

"To make it easy on you, I won't date other men, and I'll sleep in your bed every night. The rest is up to you."

Five days later, I'm watching from my kitchen window while I wash dishes.

I can hear the familiar rumble before it comes into view. "Steve, it's here!" I shout.

As I dash outside, I see the car driving toward me, a 1971 restored Karmann Ghia Volkswagen painted bright orange with original factory spec paint. The chrome bumper glistens in the sunlight.

I am sixteen. My fantasy car is in my driveway. I climb inside and inhale. The smell is identical to every VW I've ever been in. There was my mom's Beetle that I learned to drive stick in, Seth's bug that I nearly lost my virginity in, and a bus that another boyfriend drove. I've never actually been in a Karmann Ghia, but I fell in love with it when I saw Molly Ringwald driving one in *Pretty in Pink*.

My husband asks me out on a date. A first. We'll take the Ghia; it's understood.

When my father-in-law arrives to baby-sit, I'm still working on my lipstick. "Okay. I'm ready." I emerge from my bedroom, feeling beautiful and alive. My husband looks at me and smiles.

"Where are you taking me?" I ask.

"For dinner, Mexican food," he says. "I have to admit I didn't really get the car thing until I saw her," he tells me, as I pull my Ghia out of the drive.

After dinner, we stop at the grocery store and buy a pint of Häagen-Dasz ice cream with two plastic spoons. We drive to the beach and park. It's a warm night, and I ease down the passenger side window so we can listen to the surf. My husband leans over and feeds me a spoonful of chocolate chocolate chip. Then he leans over and kisses me. I feel it in every part of my body. I am sixteen.

*You can't turn back the clock.
But you can wind it up again.*

Bonnie Prudden

Michaela Galley was born an identical twin in Seattle. She earned a BA in journalism from California State University, Fresno, and is the author of a novel, The Marriage Of . . . *Michaela lives with her husband Steve and their two children in Carmel, California. She loves kickboxing, Hemingway, Steve, and cruising her '71 Ghia to the beach—not necessarily in that order.*

Why did you buy this Karmann Ghia instead of a VW Beetle?

I always thought the Ghia was more unique. A short while before I bought mine, I saw a really funky, beat-up Ghia that needed to be completely redone parked near my house with a "for sale" sign. The price was only $1,700, and although I didn't want a fixer-upper, I realized that my "dream" was within reach. I kept seeing Ghias everywhere after that—even in the movies. There was the cute yellow one with a load of cocaine in the back in *Starsky and Hutch* and the powder blue convertible Ghia in *Kill Bill Volume II.* And several times a week, I passed a restored red coupe driven by a little old lady in the neighborhood.

I researched online and found out that only about 400,000 Ghias were made in a joint effort between the German company Karmann Coachworks and Italian designer Carozzeria Ghia. My maiden name is Carozza, and it just seemed like a sign. There was a link on one of the sites for eBay. Point, click, and I found an orange Ghia that had been loved and pampered in Santa Barbara for the last twenty-five years. It was all over for me!

Tell us more about your dream car, now that you've had it for a while.

I've gotten to know all of her quirks over the last two months. Since the car and I are about the same age, mid-thirties, I'm tolerant of her imperfections. I ran out of gas the first week because the gas gauge isn't precise and the tank only holds ten gallons. But overall, she runs beautifully. I drive the car several times a week when my kids are elsewhere and I don't have to go far. My husband can't drive a stick, so for now he has to ask me out on a date if he wants a ride in my Ghia!

Has the car changed your life?

Absolutely! I live in California where the car is king, and this car really reflects my personality and fun self. When I drive my SUV or station wagon, I'm a drone worker bee and incognito. The days I drive the Ghia, I feel free, like my true self. People smile at me when I'm driving my happy, orange car.

How do you keep the sixteen-year-old in you alive?

I shop in the junior department, wear glittery tinsel nail polish, go on dates with my man, and enjoy being a girl!

Flip-Flops

❦

Diana Spechler

I never thought about marrying my brother until last December, when my parents, my sister and her husband, and my brother and I stayed a week in Nassau at a hotel I'll call Flip-Flops. Flip-Flops is in fact a chain of all-inclusive couples-only resorts that are sprinkled around the Caribbean like tropical jewels. Couples can eat fried conch and drink piña coladas until they burst, and they never have to stop being in love the whole time. In fact, couples who vacation at these resorts will be as inseparable as a pair of flip-flops—the flip-flops you fell in love with and bought years ago; that you vowed to wear for the rest of your life because you'd never find better ones; the flip-flops that are beaten-up and ugly now, but that you're so attached to, you can't bear to dispose of them.

Weeks before we were to meet in Nassau, I asked my mother, who had organized the trip, "Isn't Flip-Flops a couples resort?"

"No," she scoffed. "It's a resort for adults!"

"Are you sure?" I asked suspiciously. My mother is notorious for such mistakes. If you tell her your name is Brandon, she'll call you Brendan. She's never remembered a movie title in her life. She sends letters to me at my sister's address and vice versa.

"A resort for adults," she repeated. "No kids allowed. Won't that be nice?"

Okay, I thought several weeks later, as I wheeled my suitcase through Flip-Flops's lobby. *A resort for adults. Where every room has one canopied bed. Which I am supposed to share with my twenty-two-year-old brother Ian.*

No problem. We used to bathe together. What was the big deal about sharing a bed? But when a Flip-Flops employee in a Hawaiian shirt handed Ian and me two glasses of champagne and a little plastic beach bag full of sensual body lotions, a Howard Stern show I'd once heard emerged unsolicited from my memory: He'd interviewed a brother and sister from a club called BASIL, aka Brothers And Sisters In Love. The brother and sister talked graphically and defensively about their special brother-sister bond. Which included sex.

So as I sipped my champagne, surrounded by stone fountains shaped like dancing couples, I sidled up to the concierge and asked if she'd mind sending up a cot. When she raised her penciled eyebrows at me, I briefly looked away. Couples, sandy, barefoot, and sunburned, stood embracing on the marble floor. Others cuddled on the plush velvet love seats. Then I spotted my brother. He was chugging champagne. When he finished, he caught me looking at him and belched.

"A cot," I repeated, "for my room."

The concierge blushed and cleared her throat, then leaned forward and whispered, "Tell me your room number. I'll see what I can do."

The man behind me in line pulled his wife closer to him, as if my request for separate beds were contagious.

Please understand: I am not bitter. I don't celebrate Valentine's Day by burning pictures of my ex. I don't make gagging sounds when I drive by a bride standing outside a church on a sunny day. I believe quite firmly in love. It was just that most couples I saw that week at Flip-Flops exhibited aggressive, even competitive, affection. Some stood in the shallow end of the pool and made out. Some booked his-and-hers massages, then wandered around the resort in fluffy robes. Some wore matching wetsuits and scuba gear, then held hands underwater. It seemed that everyone at Flip-Flops was vying for the Most in Love Couple award.

"How many of these people do you think are having affairs?" I asked my sister on day two of our vacation. We were lounging by the ocean, watching couples stroll arm-in-arm along the beach.

"None," said my sister.

"None?" I laughed. "If they were secure in their marriages," I pointed out, "they wouldn't vacation at Flip-Flops."

"I'm secure in my marriage. Mom and Dad are secure in their marriage."

"But think about it," I said. "People *can't* have affairs here. What are they going to do, hit on each other's husbands and wives? We're in a safe zone. A no-cheating zone. But a different resort . . ."

"Would be more of a meat market."

"Right."

"God," she said, slathering sunscreen on her arm, "can't people just go on vacation?"

At that point, I conceded to stop assessing and obsessing and to appreciate what I had. If you thought about it, Ian and I were probably the healthiest couple on the resort. We jogged together every day. We drank Coronas together in the hot tub every evening. Afterwards, in our room, he'd patiently channel-surf while I showered and dressed so we could walk to dinner together. From his cot, he told me stories late into the night about his roller-coaster life as a college student.

But married people can sense other married people. There is a married-people club, in fact, to which every married couple on earth automatically belongs. Everywhere you turned, you'd hear, "Oh my God, we got married in October, *too*! Chris! Come here! Chris, they got married in *October*!" Giant couples cliques formed all over the resort. I felt jealous, like in sixth grade when everyone but me got a bra. So I began to pretend that Ian and I *were* a couple. When people asked where we were from, Ian would say, "Texas," and I'd just smile, instead of admitting that I lived in Wyoming. In the hot tub, I kept my hands underwater to hide my naked ring finger.

But after a few days, as our honeymoon period dwindled, I began to have doubts about my marriage to Ian. "Don't look," he'd say, when he changed for bed, "unless you want a private viewing of my enormous dick." He talked about sex. He farted in his cot. When I wanted to read and fall asleep, he wanted to watch hockey or porn. His brotherliness started to annoy me.

How would we ever be a couple if he continued to be so revolting? During the day, he'd point out women's tattooed breasts or untied bikini straps. Once, after overhearing her unmistakable accent, he struck up a conversation with a German woman in his college-level German. She stared up at him from her beach chair with disgust in her eyes.

Oh, my God, I thought. *She thinks he's my husband!*

"Hey, *Bro,*" I called, "I'm going to grab a Corona."

Ian glanced at me. "Yeah?" he said. "Well, let's have a parade."

Later, as we walked together through the resort, a young couple smiled at us, and I pushed Ian into a shrub. I got him into a headlock at every opportunity. It was cramping my style, being married to a college kid who looked just like me.

On the last evening of our vacation, I was taking a long, luxurious shower, ignoring Ian's knocks on the bathroom door. We had dinner reservations, and he was hungry, and he was sick of me spending 9,000 hours a day in the bathroom.

"I said I'm *coming!*" I shouted.

"Bet you haven't even washed your hair yet."

I squirted shampoo into my palm. "Bet you can kiss my ass."

I heard my mother enter the room. Ian told her I'd been hogging the bathroom since the fall of Rome.

She called in to me, "Meet us at Crystal Palace for dinner."

I heard the click of the door, then quickly finished washing my hair. I turned off the shower and listened. Ian hadn't really left me. Had he? I cracked the bathroom door. The hotel room was quiet, the television a silent square of black.

Outside, it was raining. I'm terrible with directions, and I hadn't learned my way around the resort yet. Supposedly, Flip-Flops had eight restaurants. We'd eaten at about five of them so far, and I didn't even know where those were. I walked around in the dark for ten minutes and wound up back where I'd started. My high-heeled sandals slipped and began carving blisters into my toes. Couples jogged by, men suspending windbreakers over women's heads. I asked a Flip-Flops employee for directions.

"You're walking?" He clucked his tongue. "You know it's not on the resort, right? Crystal Palace is a casino. Are you going gambling?"

I swallowed hard and shook my head.

"It's a ten-minute cab ride," he said, as the rain became a downpour. "You don't want to walk." He pointed to the building that housed the front desk. "Go talk to the woman in there. She'll call you a cab."

"A cab?" I had no money. The point of an all-inclusive resort is that you never need your wallet. I was confused: Why would my family eat dinner at a casino outside of the resort? And couldn't they have warned me that I'd need a cab?

At the reception desk, the concierge who had arranged for Ian's cot said I'd have to wait an hour for a taxi.

"An hour?" I felt my eyes fill with tears. It was the feeling I'd had at nineteen when my college boyfriend, an expert skier, left me in a steep, icy forest and skied easily to the bottom of the slope. I shivered, remembering that day, how after removing my skis and sidestepping down the mountain, I finally reconnected with him an hour and a half later and was shamefully ecstatic to see him, despite his having left me for dead, my nose running, my skis positioned in a terrified arrow. I was so stupid then, dating such a self-admiring testosterone vessel just so I wouldn't be alone.

I walked back into the rain, clutching my arms, rubbing my palms up and down my wet sleeves for warmth. Another Flip-Flops employee walked by in a soaking-wet Hawaiian shirt. I asked him how long the walk was to Crystal Palace.

"Why do you want to go *there*?" He laughed.

"I'm meeting my family for dinner."

"Dinner?" He frowned. "You mean the Crystal Room?" He pointed off in the distance. "That's one of our restaurants."

I hesitated for a second. It made perfect sense, of course, that my mother would call the Crystal Room "Crystal Palace."

"Probably," I said. "I'll bet that's it."

He walked me to the Crystal Room, held the door open with one arm, and sure enough, there was my family, dry and cozy, sipping white wine at three tables-for-two pushed together. There was one empty seat, beside my brother.

"Were you standing out in the rain?" my mother asked. She reached across the table to pat my hand.

"Ian abandoned me," I said, jamming an elbow into his ribs. "I got lost."

I looked around the restaurant at all the couples. They leaned into each other across tables, lovingly touching each other's faces, feeding each other grilled grouper or chocolate torte. My sister and her husband shared a menu. My parents held hands. It occurred to me all at once that Flip-Flops was a caricature of my old fears: When I was nineteen and twenty, if

I was single for a few months, I thought I was the only single person in the world. At Flip-Flops, without a husband, I really was. At least back in college, I always had single friends to commiserate with. At Flip-Flops, I was the lone soldier, marching solo through tropical sands. But what occurred to me, finally, was that I really didn't care.

I wriggled out of my wet cardigan, squeezed rain from my hair, and decided to divorce my brother. I didn't need a husband. Besides, he was all wrong for me. I looked forward to being alone the next day, to lying in the sun and finishing my book. I vowed to savor my singledom, feel grateful that I wasn't married to any of the married guys on the beach, wasn't being asked to slather sunscreen on some sweaty, hairy male back. I would enjoy the last day of my vacation, and I would look forward to my brother one day bringing home the girl who would become his wife. She could have him. I was flying solo.

It has long been my belief that in times of great stress, such as a four-day vacation, the thin veneer of family wears off almost at once, and we are revealed in our true personalities.

Shirley Jackson

Diana Spechler was a 2004–2005 Steinbeck Fellow at San Jose State University, California, the year she wrote this story. Her fiction and nonfiction have appeared in a variety of publications, including the Greensboro Review, Moment, *and* Lilith, *and on the McSweeneys' Web site. She recently won the Jerry Jazz Musician Short Story Contest, and in 2003, she won the* Madison Review's *Chris O'Malley Fiction Prize. She is at work on her first novel.*

What would be your ideal singles vacation?

I've had my ideal singles vacation several times now. My friends Jen and Aryn and I have lived in three different states for the past two years. As often as possible, two of us will fly to visit the third for a few days. We eat Pad Thai and drink red wine, and it doesn't really matter where we are because we don't do anything except talk and laugh. I can't think of anything I'd rather do. Ever. The last time we congregated, we went to Napa Valley, which basically just meant more red wine than usual and more expensive Thai food.

Ideal couples vacation?

A week in the Greek Islands. I've never been to Greece, and I know next to nothing about the Greek Islands, but I just like the way it sounds: Greek. Islands. It just has such a romantic, balmy ring to it. Doesn't it?

Tell us about the best holiday you ever took.

There are two. I once went with friends to the Sinai Peninsula, just south of Israel, and we stayed in huts on the beach and slept wrapped up in rugs. My sneakers got stolen, but I didn't mind. Another time, my sister and I joined my father on one of his business trips to India. That was about twelve years ago, and through a strange set of circumstances, we wound up staying with Deepak Chopra's parents. I don't know anyone else who has done that.

Have you gone on any family trips since Flip-Flops?

We haven't had a family vacation in a while, mostly because my sister was pregnant and then taking care of an infant. But next August, we're all going to St. John. The baby will be almost nine months old. I still haven't gotten a straight answer about whether or not we're staying at a couples resort, but I do know that my brother and I will once again be roommates.

I Want to Sing

❦

Kathy L. Reed

Aunt Ida pushed the chipped mug of hot coffee and a box of tissues to me across the Formica-topped table and sat down heavily in the chrome-backed chair. Her tarnished silver hair was piled haphazardly on top of her head and pinned with old, brown bobby pins that she kept in a cold cream jar in her top bureau drawer. Her housedress, worn thin across her ample middle by years of rubbing against countertops and the stove, was now faded, and it was hard to guess its original color. Her fingers were slightly gnarled from arthritis, but they were still the strongest hands I had ever seen.

But none of this was what you noticed first about Aunt Ida. It was her eyes, steel blue, with a depth of intensity that spoke not of the color, but of the harshness of a life that forced them to stare out at the world with understanding and determination. These eyes that had watched two of her children be buried upon the hill behind her farm, that had seen her husband

238

kissing another woman in the car when she had walked three miles to take him his lunch at the steel mill one hot summer day. These eyes.

Now they stared at me across the table with a quiet desperation to make me understand, help me somehow see what it means to live a Southern woman's life for seventy years. I needed to understand, sitting here feeling like such a total failure for not being able to "keep a man happy" and for facing signing divorce papers for the third time from another one whom I "couldn't hold" by being myself and pouring everything I had into the marriage.

"Marriage is not about love," she began. "A woman knows from the time she's born, for she is told often enough, that the best she can hope for in this life is to marry a man who can be a good provider, to endure whatever he dishes out, and to make the best of it without complaining or ever thinking about giving up." I crumbled the tissue in my hand and sniffed, thinking giving up seemed like the only option I had to keep any semblance of self-respect.

Then she leaned over and whispered, as if the entire state of Alabama would hear her and hang her down at the county courthouse for uttering the words. "One time, I wanted to be a singer. Oh, I used to sing at church; we all did that. But I got it in my head that I was good enough to sing for pay." She chuckled as if it were an absurd thought to her now, but at the same time, I saw the tears begin to well up in her eyes, tears that would never fall, for she would never allow them to. She passed me another tissue as the tears flowed freely down my cheeks, and she patted my hand with hers.

She stiffened her back against the cold metal chair and smiled. "I ran off one day. I went down to the tavern downtown and walked right in. I must have been about sixteen. I walked right up to the owner and said, 'I'm here to sing for you.'" Her eyes crinkled, and the lines there grew deeper. "He laughed and looked at me with the darkest eyes I had ever seen. I would think about those eyes many times late in the evenings for years to come. Anyway, he told the piano player to play for me, and I climbed up there on the stage and began singing my heart out. That's where I was standing when my papa came in the door. I'll never forget the look he gave me that day, like he was totally disgusted with me for not knowing my place. He beat me that night until I finally realized that it was a fool notion, and I never thought another thing about it."

I knew that wasn't true, but that it made her feel better to say it.

"I met your Uncle Hershall at church. That's where we met boys then. And he kept grinning at me the whole time the preacher was yelling and pounding his fists about the sins of the flesh and hellfire and damnation. There sat Hershall, grinning."

I knew this part of the story, about her marrying Hershall simply because he was the only one who asked. About his years of drinking and her finally scraping together enough money for them to buy a house of their own, a two-room home on the edge of Charlotte's Hill. And how, by the next year, the bank had foreclosed on it because Hershall had run off again with another woman and she couldn't pay the bills with him gone. I knew he had come back, and she had taken him back without a word.

"I did what I had to," she said quietly.

The pain I felt as I listened to her choked me, and I wondered how much of it was pain and how much of it was sheer terror for realizing that, forty-five years later, I was doing no better, not because of lack of choices, but from years of receiving the same conditioning she had. Now I sat across from her, thirty years younger and not nearly as strong, and heard the same messages playing in my head that she had heard her whole life: *Girls don't need college. Find a nice boy and marry him. If you don't have enough to keep you busy, have a baby.*

The only time I had ever seen pride in my daddy's eyes for me was the time someone told him what a good cook I was and how nice I kept my house. It wasn't when I graduated from college with honors. He thought that was a foolish waste of money. *What good is an education if you can't find a man to marry you?*

I looked at Aunt Ida, but I didn't see her. I saw me. I took her hand and said, "I want to sing. I want to sing and shout and yell if I'd like! I want to tell the people of the South that the men I've picked never did anything for me except make me feel like I was a fool for giving in to the feeling that without a man by my side I was nothing. I don't have to be dependent on a man. I can take care of myself and be happy without one."

I blew my nose and straightened in my chair. I felt like I finally had some peace with my decision to give that low-down man his walking papers.

She stared at me like I was from another planet, like these thoughts had never, ever crossed her own mind. They were not allowed to be thought and surely not allowed to be voiced. She did the only thing she knew to do. "Honey, hush. Someone will hear you. They'll surely think you've lost yo' mind."

I pushed away from the table, sighed, leaned and gave her a big hug, and slowly rinsed out my coffee mug in the chipped porcelain sink. I looked out the kitchen window with its peeling white paint and loose shutter and saw the fields that stood barren as far as my eyes could see. Something heavy hung in the air, and I felt her stare before I turned.

Those steel blue eyes were piercing me, and I looked deeply into them and finally saw it. She knew. She felt it. She understood. And she was applauding inside. We were of the same mind, the same heart. All of us were. Mama, Grandma, the sad-looking divorced lady who worked at the dress shop downtown, the lady professor I had in college who kept the bottle in her desk, my sister with her three grown kids, who never allowed her husband of thirty years to know what size she wore or that she sometimes took a nap during the day when he was gone. We were all sisters. Southern sisters.

And I knew that times could change. It wouldn't be easy or fast or without pain. But if I stood up for myself and made a choice to sign those divorce papers and hold my head up high, it would come. And I knew Aunt Ida wanted it for me and for the women who came after me, even more than I did.

To really ask is to open the door to the whirlwind.
The answer may annihilate the question and the questioner.

Anne Rice

Kathy L. Reed is a writer and former high school mathematics teacher who resides with her husband, Bruce, in Decatur, Alabama. She has four children. Being a Southern native, she cherishes her memories of the strong Southern women in her family, and they inspire much of her writing.

Since this fateful day with Aunt Ida, have you truly found your voice as an independent woman?

That day was a turning point because I think I finally learned, through that conversation, that I have to choose what is right for me, even when the decisions are hard. I've continued through the years to find my "voice" and to "sing" whenever given the opportunity. I can't please everyone. I know I will continue to make mistakes, but I will learn from them and become wiser in the process, just as Aunt Ida did, even though she'd never admit it out loud. I've learned that even by myself and even when it seems the whole world is against me, I can be okay. And to me, that's true independence. I just wish it hadn't taken me so long to get here! And it's nice to have a good man in my life whom I chose because I wanted to be with him, not because I thought I couldn't make it without him.

Have you been able to pass this independent nature along to your female children?

Yes, my daughter, Cindy, is very independent. I think some of that came from motherly advice through the years and some by watching me fall down, only to get up and make a different choice. She's happy to just do her own thing. And I love it that she's so confident. I also think with each generation, asserting ourselves as women gets a little easier.

Tell us about some of the other strong Southern women in your family who have influenced your life.
My mother made some difficult choices in her own life, getting divorced during the sixties and standing up to the enormous criticism of that decision. In doing so, she taught me that my happiness meant something, too, and that I could never please everyone regardless of my choices. Aunt Ida always told me that the choices in life would either "make you or break you, so listen to your heart and not to other people's mouths and use your head for something besides keeping your ears apart!"

Where is Aunt Ida now?
Aunt Ida has passed away. She taught me so many things. Even though she thought she had made the easy choices rather than standing up for herself, I think she had such strength to keep her spunk and humor through all of her hardships. When she was dying, she was still giving advice, telling us we'd better not be "worrying over her" because she was definitely going to a better place. I have no doubt she did.

Double Happiness

❃

Carla Gericke

It's a bitterly cold December day; it's snowing, sleeting, and raining. When it's not snowing, sleeting, or raining, it's hailing. And the wind is howling. One thing no one tells you about winters in New York: They suck. They particularly suck when you're pounding the pavement five days before your current lease expires *and* you have quit your job *and* you have forgotten your umbrella *and* you are trapped in a flurricane of snow, sleet, rain, hail, and wind.

You could be in a toasty office right now, I think, as I tug my foot from a pile of snow. My boot stays behind. Reaching down in an unstable balancing stick pose, I wonder why I thought giving up my legal career was such a smart move. *Now, here you are, trying to find a cheap place to live, so that you can, what, suffer for your art?*

The wind gusts, and I lose my balance. To prevent a head-first dive, I plant my shoeless foot. Marvelous. Now my sock is soaked. I grab the boot and cram my foot in.

Only two more, I tell myself, waiting for the light to change. Both are in the East Village. One, supposedly a loft with a garden, is located in the avenues. The other is near Tompkins Square Park.

The light turns green. Sock squishing, I huff across the intersection. Sleet pelts my face. Here's an idea for the Weather Channel: brutally frank reporting, the Tell-It-Like-It-Is Weather Report presented by I-Botox Jane and Yes-It's-A-Toupee Jim.

"Today, the weather will suck ass, Jim. No, not merely suck, that was yesterday's forecast. Today, it will really, truly *suck ass.*"

Luke, my husband, has tasked me with finding our new apartment. I suspect it's his revenge for my brazen plan to follow my bliss. Since our current lease is ending, we need to downscale to a place we can afford on one salary.

This isn't easy.

Manhattan is bloody expensive, and the apartments are ridiculously small. You have to be snappy; any offering that's mildly habitable is nabbed on the day it's listed.

Even I, a South African immigrant, know bang for your buck is The American Way. But not in New York's rental market. Here, "Spacious, sunny one-bedroom apartment for $1,850," is code for "Roach-infested crack house in dodgy neighborhood. Landlord willing to trade rent for sex."

As I scurry through the streets of Alphabet City, I recall the neighborhood maxim: *A is for Assault, B is for Battery, C is for Coma, and D is for Death.*

The loft is on Avenue D.

A birdlike woman with the bluish tint of a shut-in shows me into a long, narrow room. Her blond wig is askew. The "loft," a fourth floor walk-up, has an abnormally low ceiling, as though Munchkins or Oompa-Loompas once lived here.

"To get to the private roof garden," she explains, pointing to a window behind the kitchen sink, "you have to go through there."

Apparently, in order to get to the "garden," you have to climb into the kitchen sink, hoist open the window, swing your legs over the sill, tilt forward in the hopes that gravity will levitate your butt from the sink and onto the Astroturf, all while trying to avoid making rapturous love to the faucet.

"It's a hop, skip, and a jump," the batty landlady offers, hopping and nodding merrily. She hops and nods again, closing in on where I'm about to plop a leg in the sink.

A different course of action seems advisable.

"Must dash." I make a break for the door. Over my shoulder, I notice she is incorporating the dash into her routine.

Hop, nod, dash. Hop, nod, dash.

At the door, I pause for a moment. She slides across the floor toward me and sinks into a curtsy. It strikes me then: She looks exactly like a Smurf.

I turn and run. No curtain calls for her today.

As I trek through a deserted Tompkins Square Park toward number two, I keep my icy fingers crossed that I have depleted my daily allotment of New York loonies. I mull over the other ads from this morning. There was one somewhere downtown that had sounded vaguely promising. Rifling through my handbag, I remove my cell phone and the printout. I scan it. It sounds suspicious in the "horny landlord" way, but I call anyway. You do not turn down 1,000-plus square feet in New York. Not even if it *is* in Chinatown. Mr. Carter, "But call me 'Cart,'" invites me to come over "whenever"—he coughs between tokes—"whatever."

Hanging up, I ring the buzzer of the place near the park. This two-bedroom duplex sounded lovely, and for once, the apartment is genuinely delightful. Floors, windows, ceilings, all exactly where they should be. There's a skylight, two bathrooms—*two*—and an exposed brick fireplace. An actual door leads to a private deck overlooking the park.

Yet this place is a different kind of torture. We can't afford it.

"You want to *write?*" Luke's shocked words reverberate through my mind. "That's great, but it'll mean big changes. Belt-tightening until you get established. We're going to have to figure out a budg—"

"Don't say it." I'd grimaced. I hated that word.

As I look around, I remind myself: *To follow your dream, you have to make sacrifices.* Glancing at the study upstairs, I sigh. This is the perfect apartment, except it's almost $1,500 over the you-know-what.

So why am I here? To test my moral resolve. In the matter of *Cesspits You Can Afford vs. Gorgeous, Livable Real Estate*, the verdict is swift: Sell your soul, girl. Get back on the gravy train. No? Are you crazy? Evidently, yes. But, if I want to change careers, I'll just have to adjust my expectations down. Way, way down.

With this in mind, I struggle south toward Chinatown. Wanting to let "Cart" know I'm nearby, I dig out my cell phone.

It's dead. Of course, it is. The weather has turned into an honest to God, I-ain't-kiddin'-you-this-is-BAD-Jim blizzard.

I stop at a phone booth on a corner where I've never been before. Squinting through the snow, I think it's possibly a corner where no *gweilo* has ever been before. Things are looking up.

"Where you hangin'?" says Cart.

"I don't know."

"Can you see the bridge?"

I can't see the cradle of the phone in front of me.

"Walk toward the bridge. Look for a yellow and green thingama—Number Ninety-Nine. Pad's on the third floor."

"Buzzer number?"

I think I hear a snort. Things are definitely looking up.

When not under whiteout conditions, Chinatown's streets teem with elderly question-marks pushing battered trolleys, sidewalk fish markets, enterprising live snail merchants and, I venture to guess, *unauthorized* Louis Vuitton vendors. While the neighborhood has potential *and* great food, Chinatown is still, for me, on the wrong side of Slum Street.

The yellow-and-green awning reads "Pho 99 Happy Happy Restaurant." I hurry in through the open door, tripping over a man selling counterfeit DVDs. Under a sign for Lucky Chiang Auto Driving School, I shake off the storm and glance up, trying to get a sense of the building. The stairs are steep and filthy, but dry. At least the roof doesn't leak.

Cart is waiting on the landing. He looks more respectable than I expect him to, sort of like Einstein toward the end. From his lackadaisical speech, I was anticipating whacko, acid-fried, aging hippie in a bad way. He's more whacko, acid-fried, aging hippie in a good way.

He leads me into the apartment.

I choke, amazed at the space before me. "Have many people come over?"

"Some folks left messages. Said they'd be by tomorrow. But no one's seen it yet."

Thank you oh ye gods of suck-ass weather.

Cart leaves me to lollygag, and I like him for it. Finding a home is an intensely personal experience. I want to sniff about, open and close doors and drawers. I need to visualize how our furniture will look. I need time to absorb the atmosphere. Study the light. Check for rat poop.

The floor is divided into two apartments, with Cart's smaller one in the rear. He moved in twenty years ago, long before the area was swallowed by the Red Dragon. For the past few years, Cart tells me, a bunch of moochers have inhabited *my* loft.

There are four large windows with an unobstructed view of the Manhattan Bridge. I picture myself at my desk near the window. I imagine bright sunlight streaming in. I turn my face into the chimerical sunshine—it's warm on my skin.

There are, just as the ad claimed, two bedrooms. *This will be our room,* I point as I pirouette around the massive living area, *and that will be Luke's den.*

There's ample space for our oversized furniture. The walls beg for our eclectic art. For an apartment within the budget— even if there's a guy downstairs hawking Kung-Fu porno in the lobby—this is the best deal ever.

"I'll take it," I say. I'm practically prancing.

Later, after discussing my discovery with Luke, I review the four-page contract Cart e-mailed over. He has written the lease himself, which makes me nervous. It's impossible for any attorney to resist the temptation to fiddle with a contract, especially one written by a layperson. And if that layperson looks like he might own a bong or two? Doubly so. My lawyerly instinct immediately raises its ugly control-freak head. *Down, girl,* I admonish it. *This is about a residential space sandwiched between a driving school and a single occupancy hotel that may or may not be a house of ill repute, remember? You're a writer now, not a lawyer. Let it slide.* I force myself to keep an open mind as the words wash over me. Suddenly, I don't care what it says. *What's the worst that can happen if I just sign it as is?*

I smile and continue to read until I reach the last paragraph. It says: "You can stay as long as you don't mess with my ability to enjoy life, liberty, and the pursuit of happiness." I burst out laughing.

I can dig it, man.

Without changing a word, I print it and scribble my signature next to "Tenant."

If Cart wants to pursue happiness, jolly good. So do I.

What's that lucky Chinese symbol called? Double Happiness? From now on, that's what I plan to pursue. In a loft on Slum Street, above the Happy Happy Restaurant and the Lucky Chiang Driving School, sitting near the window, with sunshine on my face, I'll be writing.

The greatest part of our happiness depends on our dispositions, not our circumstances.

Martha Washington

Carla Gericke lives with her husband and one sad cactus in a decrepit loft in Chinatown, New York City. She was born in South Africa, raised by diplomats, and later moved to the United States. When not writing, she tutors at 826NYC, a literacy program for little monsters. Her work has appeared or is forthcoming in a variety of online and print publications, including Wild Strawberries, Pindeldyboz, SL Magazine, *and* Underground Voices. Her story "The Mighty Zuluman" won first place in AIM's 2004 short story contest.

What did your husband think of the place?

Luke loved the space, but was skeptical about the layout. Imagine a long, rectangular shape divided into three parts. The big chunk in the front is our unit, and the little one at the back is Cart's. In between, there's a "no man's land" which contains Cart's kitchen and four doors: the communal front door, the two doors leading to the separate units, and, strangely, the door to our private bathroom. Basically, our bathroom is outside our apartment, off Cart's kitchen, which, for reasons unknown, is not inside his apartment. Yes, I admit, an interesting design.

So, on occasion, while Cart is cooking his breakfast, I'm dashing around in my wet towel, scrambling through the Egg Zone toward the safe house. At first, it seemed a tad odd, but now we jokingly refer to it as "the outhouse."

As of now, how long have you lived there?
We've been in "The Knickerbocker" for one year, five months, nineteen days, but who's counting? We're very happy here and hope to stay for a long time.

The Knickerbocker?
You know how the swanky, doormen buildings in New York have posh names? Well, even though we were the proud renters of an outhouse, we decided our building deserved a name, too. The post office down the street is called "Knickerbocker," and since Luke and I are both of Dutch descent, we thought, If the wooden shoe fits . . .

How has your perspective on the neighborhood changed?
Chinatown is fascinating. Luke and I are well traveled, adventurous, and have lived in unusual locations, like India. Living here also feels like living in a foreign, third-world country. It's crowded and dirty, I don't understand the languages spoken around me, I can't read the store signs, but in this little pocket of Manhattan, I have the best of all worlds. I'm both in New York and in China. It no longer feels like Slum Street. It feels like my street. I'm proud to be part of this community.

How has downshifting worked out for you?

It astounds me daily how satisfying a creative career is. It sounds trite, but I'm a much happier person and hopefully a better wife, daughter, sister, and friend. I've started cooking and am conquering world cuisine, one region at a time. I tutor at a youth literacy program and am starting a writers workshop. At times, it can be a challenge. For me, the hardest part was learning to cope with rejection slips. But what doesn't kill you . . . right? We hope to start a family soon, and being far from home, it's good to know we have a built-in baby-sitter named Cart.

So things are working out well with Cart?

Er, yes. Cart's big-hearted and intelligent, a wonderful photographer, the best landlord I have ever had, and an absolute character. For example: before we moved in, I questioned him about crime in the neighborhood. He said: "In all my time here, I have never been robbed." Okay, great. Soon after we'd settled in, I invited him over for dinner, and he regaled us with tales of the neighborhood: gang warfare during the eighties, an illegal gambling house on the roof during the early nineties, the time the FBI crashed down the door in search of a drug den. Then, casually, he mentioned the time he "almost fell over a corpse on the landing." What? Of course, the neighborhood is much safer now, but I did learn a lesson. When inquiring about residential crime statistics, be thorough: Burglaries? Check. Opium dens? Check. Dead people? Check.

What brought you to the United States from South Africa?

As unbelievable as it may seem, I won a green card in the lottery. Americans are often amazed to discover the U.S. government holds an annual lottery to bestow green cards on foreigners. At the time, in 1993, I was still in law school. Luke and I were dating, and we'd just moved in together. Of approximately 24 million applicants, 25,000 worldwide winners would be randomly selected. With those odds, we entered as a lark.

Then I won!

After completing enough paperwork to destroy a good portion of the earth's rain forests, the U.S. Consulate in Johannesburg scheduled an interview with me. A stern, bespectacled government agent seated behind six inches of bulletproof glass barked questions at me over a microphone. A spotlight was trained on my face. There was no air-conditioning on my side of the booth. Late into the interrog— interview, I rather naively asked whether Luke would be getting a green card, too. From behind the glass, the voice boomed: "Either you get married, or you go alone. Next!"

Faced with this ultimatum, we did the only thing we could. We eloped.

Of course, it was an emotional decision to leave South Africa. Nelson Mandela had just been released from jail, the first free and fair elections would soon take place, our families remained, but I felt winning the green card meant I was destined to a different future. Carpe diem! Seizing opportunities has led me on wonderful adventures, for which I'm grateful.

Following Anaïs

❦

Cynthia W. Gentry

I'm sitting in Café Borrone in Menlo Park, staring at the cursor on my computer screen. On my right, some guy drones on and on about second-round funding and customer touchpoints. Nearby, an au pair entertains her friends with a loud, nonstop monologue in rapid-fire German. On my left, a woman with a perfect blonde ponytail and a Hermès scarf yammers about a charity fundraiser. Little do they know that next to them, I'm writing an orgy scene so hot it would make them choke on their cappuccinos.

I rest my face in my hands and stare at my screen. Briefly, I imagine turning to the society matron and asking her if she knows any good metaphors for the clitoris. I quickly discard the idea. It's not so much that I'm afraid of shocking her, although I'd rather not get thrown out of this café. It's just that I try to avoid corny, romance-novel metaphors for genitalia whenever possible. That's just the kind of sex writer I am.

That's right. I have become, somewhat inadvertently, a writer of erotica. Porn. Whatever you want to call it. Instead of writing the Great American Novel, I'm trying to figure out how to describe two men having sex with two women at a tantric *puja* (that's a big circle of people having sex, for those of you not up on your tantric ritual) in the forest while their hosts go at it on a raised dais for everyone to see. Talk about your customer touchpoints.

I didn't set out to become an erotica writer, although anyone who knew about the Barbie-doll nudist camps I staged as a child might disagree. But through most of my childhood, teen, and college years, I remained relatively innocent, without even a serious boyfriend until I was twenty-two, a boyfriend I then proceeded to marry. So how did I become a woman who found herself advising the readers of a major men's magazine that a plastic-wrapped electric toothbrush can, in a pinch, double as a vibrator?

Flash back to 1991. I had been married for almost four years, and living in Sunnyvale, a pleasant but pathologically uneventful suburb in the San Francisco Bay Area. My marriage, though amiable, was foundering. My libido had decided to take a vacation; I considered putting "missing" ads for it on milk cartons.

This was, to make an understatement, troubling. Because I liked sex. A lot. After losing my virginity somewhat disastrously my freshman year at a dorm party and experiencing a few more episodes of deeply unsatisfying carnal relations, I had met my husband and discovered what all the fuss was about.

But as the years passed, my libido ebbed away like air leaking out of a tire, and I found myself limping along in a marriage that had started out like a sexy convertible sports car and now more closely resembled a Yugo on its last legs. When we'd been dating, I had been so wild for my husband that we could only make it as far as the back seat of the car. Now, his kisses left me cold. I tried to blame antidepressants, but deep down, I knew they weren't the sole cause.

I'll save the analysis of "what went wrong in my marriage" for another time. Suffice to say, resentment—most commonly produced by finding yourself turned into your spouse's mother, with responsibility for housecleaning, budgeting, shopping, and socializing while he spends hours shut in a room playing guitar—is not an aphrodisiac.

Unfortunately, it wasn't just my sexual desire that dried up. My desire to write—a constant over the previous decades—disappeared, too.

Around this time, my husband and I went with another couple to see the Philip Kaufman movie *Henry & June,* about the ménage à trois between the writer Henry Miller, his wife June, and the writer Anaïs Nin. I sat in the darkened theater entranced, longing to transport myself back to Paris in the 1920s. Coming out of the theater, I turned to my friends.

"What did you think?" I asked.

The husband shuddered. "Two hours with selfish people cheating on each other. Hated it."

"But, the acting was great, I thought." I wanted to talk about the psychology, the fantasy, the entire milieu. I hated myself for being so lame.

Undeterred, I began reading everything of Nin's I could find, and then I discovered that she had written erotica during a time when she needed money. I read *Delta of Venus* and *Little Birds*. I was intrigued.

With those first two slim volumes, I lost my literary cherry, and my libido began to stir. Then I discovered erotica anthologies, which at about that time began entering the mainstream. I bought *The Best American Erotica 1993*. I began to have erotic fantasies, lots of them. My libido had started to reappear, although sadly, my attraction for my husband didn't. Let's just say I spent many nights with my eyes closed, imagining George Clooney.

However, my desire to write had not reappeared. Writing was a chore. I was in a monthly screenwriting workshop, but with each session, I brought in less and less. I started a novel, wrote about fifty pages, and then lost interest. I wrote stories about unhappy relationships, but none of them featured so much as a kiss.

Then one night, I got sick of myself. I don't know what set me off. My husband was in his study, playing guitar. I had done the dishes. I had paid the bills. I didn't feel like watching TV. Since this was before the Internet, I couldn't surf the Web.

"What the hell," I thought. "I'll write up one of my fantasies."

I had no deadline. Nobody waiting to see what I was going to write. Nobody who was *going* to see what I was going to write. I decided to write something simply to entertain myself. Or, to be perfectly honest, to arouse myself. I didn't care if it was good or bad. I just wanted to play.

I sat down to write my fantasy just as I had imagined it, over and over, night after night. The words began to flow from me again, like those days in my childhood when writing *was* play. Several hours and 3,000 words later, I discovered that my so-called writer's block was gone.

With my libido and my writing intertwined, I began to write more stories, just for me. Most of them stayed on my computer, but I showed a few—including that first one—to friends, who showed them to their friends. I finally realized what I had done to my reputation at a dinner party one night. As soon as the host introduced me to one of his friends, a big smile crept over my new acquaintance's face.

"Oh! *You're* the pornographer!" he said.

"Ha," was my weak reply. "I guess I am. Ha ha."

Yes, my refound creativity had consequences. As I started writing again and *feeling* again, I became less satisfied with being unsatisfied. I got tired of complaining about my dead-end corporate job. Finally, I quit to start my own business. And a few months later, after years of couples therapy, I realized that my marriage was over. I had changed, but my dear husband (and he is a dear, sweet man) hadn't. I couldn't stay just because I didn't want to hurt him, and so I moved out.

Then I began a new chapter, literally. I started a graduate program in creative writing. Sex infused everything I wrote. Drawing from my own experiences as a newly single woman, I wrote a lot about comically bad sex or, after a particularly scarring breakup, tragically good sex. I still didn't consider myself a sex author—much less a "pornographer"—because I was trying to amuse and move people, not arouse them. I was a *Real Author.*

Until, of course, a publisher friend approached me to write the erotica for a book on tantric sex. Now, I knew nothing about tantric sex. But did it matter? No. A real byline dangled in front of me, and all I could think was that I'd be a *Published Writer.* So I wrote that book in about five months, and when my publisher friend asked me to write a book of 365 sex tips, I said yes to that as well.

And that's how I found myself in that café, brow furrowed, face occasionally buried in my hands. I'm sure I looked like any other writer. I didn't sit there heaving and blushing and sighing as my fingers pecked away. In fact, like most writers I know, I spent a lot of time staring into space. But instead of puzzling over how to describe a particularly interesting landscape, I was puzzling over how to describe a particularly athletic sexual position. But puzzles like that made me a better writer.

As I racked up the hours hunched over my laptop and latte, I thought of something Anaïs Nin once said: "And the day came when the risk to remain tight in a bud was more painful than the risk it took to blossom." When I took the chance of writing out that fantasy so many nights ago, I proved her right. I became more willing to take risks like starting my own business and leaving my marriage—risks that led others to tell me, "I wish I were as brave as you." But I never considered myself brave. I just did what I had to do, and my life blossomed in unimaginable ways.

❧

I can always be distracted by love, but eventually
I get horny for my creativity.

Gilda Radner

Cynthia W. Gentry is the author of The Bedside Orgasm Book: 365 Days of Sexual Ecstasy *(Fair Winds Press, 2005) and coauthor of* Red Hot Tantra: Erotic Secrets of Red Tantra for Intimate, Soul-to-Soul Sex and Ecstatic, Enlightened Orgasms *(Fair Winds Press, 2004). Even when she's not producing stories that she can't show her family, she loves to write about the crazy things that men and women do to each other. Her work has appeared in numerous literary publications, including* Area i, *the* Montserrat Review, *and* Reed Magazine, *as well as magazines such as* Budget Savvy. *She is currently at work on a novel and several screenplays. Portions of this story appeared previously on* SFStation.com.

How's your love life since you left your husband?

Well, I certainly had some dating adventures after my divorce, although a good portion of them veered toward tragi-comic. Finally, though, I started enjoying being single and meeting different people. And wouldn't you know it? It was then that I met a wonderful man who was not only ten years my junior, but my neighbor. At first, I was reluctant to date him, but it wasn't the age difference: I just didn't want somebody watching my comings and goings from three doors down. But soon he won me over with his humor, wisdom, and kindness, and now we're engaged.

How does he like being engaged to a sex writer?

He does get a lot of mileage from it at parties. But despite what people think, we're not trying out Kama Sutra poses every night.

We have a passionate, close, loving relationship, and I feel very blessed.

Would you share a bit of what you wrote that night?
No, because it would reveal too much about me! Let's just say that I wanted to explore the idea of a "male escort"—something a little taboo, since normally it's the other way around. I guess the story worked because one of my gay friends told me it got him hot even though it portrayed heterosexual sex.

What are your top three metaphors for genitalia?
I can only pick three? I like the terms used in ancient Chinese pillow books, like "Jade Stem" for the male organ and "Jade Pavilion" for female genitalia. And then there's the lovely "Pearl on the Jade Step" for the clitoris. I think these names are much more evocative than some of our Western phrases, which are too flowery, too vague, or just plain tacky.

Stark Raving Mom

Veronica Chater

Family life has a way of sneaking up on you. The other day, I was shocked to realize that I am a wife, the mother of three boys, that I drive a minivan, hold a steady job, and that our monthly overhead is more than I used to earn in six months in my twenties. And that somewhere in the process, I forgot how to have fun.

When was the last time I stayed out all night? Or behaved irresponsibly? Or got drunk? Or laughed till I cried? My definition of fun had changed so radically, it wasn't in the same dictionary anymore. Now "fun" meant what Mommy can do with finger-paints and glue or how high Mommy can build a bubble crown on her kids' heads during bath time. At the rate I was going, "fun" would soon mean warming a seat at the bingo club or having brunch at the senior center.

It was an emergency. I had to seize the day before the day was gone. But what could I do? There was only one thing I could think of. Call my hip younger sister Bernadette. So I did.

"What are you doing this weekend?" I asked.

"Going to a rave in San Francisco. Wanna come?"

"What time can you pick me up?"

It was nine o'clock at night when Bernadette and her friends, average age twenty-two, arrived dressed in halter tops and pigtails. Taking one look at me, Bernadette said, "You're not ready!" She yanked me by the hand into the bathroom and applied my "candy" (face glitter, tattoos, plastic jewelry, etc.) until I sparkled like a preschool fairy queen. My boys watched, wide-eyed and impressed.

"You look pretty, Mommy," Kyle said.

Laughing and only a little embarrassed, I kissed John and the boys goodbye and climbed into Portia's car—a small Japanese vehicle with a bumper sticker that read, "Just say no to sex with pro-lifers." Portia, Bernadette's best friend, set her multiple CD player to shuffle. Track 12 opened to whale calls synched with computerized percussion. And we drove off. Fast.

Soon we were flying across the Bay Bridge on our way to a shopping center in the Castro, where a guy in a red jacket outside of Jamba Juice was supposed to give us directions.

In the center of the back seat, I braced myself and tried to remain calm. Suddenly, I felt very vulnerable, a little lost in time, a tiny bit lost to myself, and extremely dependent on Portia's driving. What was I doing? Why was I here?

Something about driving 85 mph in a rockin' and stompin' little car at night prompts you to locate yourself in your particular box in time. My box is quite small and rigidly built. It contained our recent home addition that lasted over a year and drove us all insane. I brought cups of coffee to the carpenters every morning and watched them cut our roof off and throw it into a Dumpster in our front yard. They jack-hammered our foundation out from under us and tore off the wood siding while the kids watched *Barney* and *Sesame Street* over the noise and built forts with the couch cushions. It contained Kyle's night frights, Daniel's recurring asthma, and Cameron's ear infections that required frequent emergency room visits. It contained my job with its incessant deadlines, the drudgery of housework, and the permanent obligation to cook. My box made me feel extremely indispensable, but also extremely restricted.

Julie, on my left, and Bernadette, on my right, didn't have boxes with tangible perimeters. They were girls dancing—fully dancing—in their seats on their way to a rave where they'd lose themselves completely in wide, open space. *Look Mom! No perimeters!* In front, Portia and Auzzie were both fully dancing in their seats, too, and I'm not exaggerating.

"There he is," Portia said, pointing to our Jamba Juice contact.

"Sweet," said Bernadette.

At home, John would be reading *Go, Dog, Go.* Cameron would be cherry-cheeked, Kyle would be looking doughy and droopy, and Daniel, who just lost his two front teeth, would be whistling through the gap and acting too sophisticated for *Go, Dog, Go.* After the book, they'd brush their teeth, dash to their rooms, and wrestle on the floor for a few minutes, procrastinating the inevitable. By then, John would be snapping at them, "In bed, boys! Before I have to count! Okay! I'm counting! One . . . Two . . ."

Auzzie got directions from the red jacket, and we headed to South of Market, where we pulled into a parking lot. The doors flew open, and the whale music echoed inside the concrete structure. Portia and Julie danced by the car. Portia's pigtails stuck straight out as she swung her head around and around like a human propeller, and Julie looked as if she were running in place on a speedy treadmill. Bernadette and Auzzie began doing tai chi in the middle of the parking lot. I stood alone. They took no notice of me. Why should they notice me? I was a mother. I had enormous responsibilities: a mortgage, building inspections, baby well-checks, mammograms, PTA meetings. But that's deep, too, they seemed to say. *I mean, really. No discrimination.*

We left the parking lot and walked up Market Street (Portia still dancing), turned right on 5th, and walked three blocks to an old Victorian house where a big bouncer-type guy was leaning against a wrought-iron gate. We showed him our tickets and walked two flights up a ratty wooden staircase to a big room.

Inside, the air was tepid and smoky and jammed with people. Everyone was dancing. All around, the bare bellies and flare-legs looked vaguely familiar, like we were on the set of a seventies sitcom. I had to remind myself that I was in the twenty-first century and moving forward fast and that my own kids were on the tail end of this generation, so I'd better pay attention if I wasn't going to be left behind.

The music playing was called trance house. I liked it. It certainly outdid *A Tisket, A Tasket* or *Hey Diddle Diddle.* The rhythm was bouncing off the walls as fast paced as a rapid-fire machine gun. It entered my bloodstream and vibrated through my body, making my nervous system feel like it was on Pop Rocks. It was impossible not to dance.

And so I danced.

And danced.

And danced.

For what seemed a lifetime, but wasn't even close. At around midnight, I looked at my watch and wondered how much longer we were going to stay. But by the look of things, the party was only just beginning to pick up. People were still arriving. A shadowy figure with a hood asked if I needed E or O. Smiling awkwardly, I said (sounding very much like my mother), "Thank you very much, but not just now." He smiled cynically and wandered away. I shrank inside and decided to go find some fresh air.

Slipping through "security," I walked up a couple of flights of stairs to the roof and looked out over San Francisco. It was a beautiful, clear night. The traffic was a medium flow as people headed home after their evening's entertainment—probably to the theater or the symphony. Not like us. Up here, I stood beside a line of pigeons that were huddled in the gutters. Beside me, a circle of guys were rapping and mouth popping. Their lyrics exposed their disillusionment with the establishment. Deep down, I knew that I represented everything they couldn't bear. But like them, I felt trapped in my reality. A reality I couldn't escape.

I knew that Cameron would get up that morning at six-thirty or seven o'clock and stand by our bed and say, "Get up now, Mommy. It's morning time." That likelihood alone stopped me from drinking or taking any drugs, or doing anything dangerous like standing too close to the edge of the roof, or allowing anyone besides myself to drive home. I even admit to noticing the extension cords running along the walls downstairs and thinking, *This place is a fire hazard.* I had to snap out of it. I reminded myself that I'd come to dance, and that's what I was going to do.

Walking back downstairs, I swam back into the smoky biosphere of black lights and neon sticks and kissing and back-rubbing girls and forced myself to move to the machine-gun rhythm of the music. But my feet were aching and I was developing a headache, so five minutes later, I slunk to a quiet corner and leaned against the wall.

"It's no use," I sighed to myself. I used to have the kind of energy it took to dance the entire night, but I was realizing that fun is a relative thing. If you were a mom, it was something that happened in the wakeful hours of the day. Writing a letter to a friend, watching the kids learn to swing, making bread, planting tomatoes, and going to bed at ten o'clock with a cup of tea and a book. Dancing might be fun for an hour, but after four hours, it seemed like a stubborn exercise in sweat-manufacturing.

The hours began to drag. Blurry-eyed, yawning, and bored, I began to suspect that what had begun as an innocent adventure in self-discovery was turning out to be a disco black hole. In this room, it felt as if real life didn't exist anymore. Like there was no day on the other side of this feel-good night. No world beyond these brick walls. No air, no water. No human enterprise, no social structure, no loving family. I'd entered an orgiastic *Twilight Zone.*

Hours later, as I blinked away the dryness in my eyes, I suddenly noticed a thin flag of daylight on the west-facing wall, a beautiful ghost that signaled that there was, in fact, life beyond these walls. Elated, I gestured to Bernadette, who was still working out on the dance floor, that I'd be waiting for them outside. She nodded, but kept dancing. The music was still going strong. Why would anyone want to leave?

In the chilly dawn, I breathed in the wonderfully brisk, oxygen-rich air, and watched a garbage truck making its slow trip up the street. It wasn't until it had passed me and turned the corner that my sister and her friends emerged from the iron-gated door and we headed for home. I was so thrilled to be driving back over the bridge that I went through an invigorating second wind and enjoyed the gray dawn over the bay.

In my mind, I could hear the sound of Cameron and Kyle dumping the toy box out in the middle of the living room floor and sliding down the wooden stairs on bath towels. The little *Thomas the Tank* was burning out its battery as it strained against a couch leg. Daniel was putting a piece of bread in the toaster. It slowly turned black while he took his time locating the jam in the fridge, then conclusively dropped the jam jar onto the tile floor. The jar broke noisily into a thousand sticky shards just as I wafted through the front door, a thick cloud of stale smoke hovering around me, and fell backwards onto the couch.

"Mommy's home!" they shouted, piling on top of me and smothering me with vigorous kisses. Laughing, I held onto them and squeezed for all I was worth, but when their noses registered my stale stench, they let go and ran away squealing, "Mommy stinks!"

Fun. Chaos. Parenthood. And it was the extraordinary beginning of another day.

To live is so startling it leaves little time for anything else.

Emily Dickinson

Veronica Chater was born in San Francisco. As the second oldest of eleven children in a strict Catholic family, she had the responsibilities of a mother at the age of twelve. Her childhood passion for writing led to a career as a magazine writer and essayist. She has published more than 100 feature articles, personal essays, and creative nonfiction stories in over a dozen magazines and newspapers in the United States and England. She is a regular contributor on NPR's This American Life. *Her first novel,* Vespers Nine, *is represented by the Castiglia Literary Agency and is on submission to publishers.*

Any exciting adventures since rave night?
Yes! John surprised me with a fabulous gift for my birthday. We went out for breakfast, and he gave me a beautifully wrapped package tied with ribbons and a big bow. I shook it and said, "It's just about the weight of a blender. Oh, honey. You really shouldn't have." Then I opened the present, and it was a helmet and a set of Vespa keys. The Vespa was parked in the restaurant parking lot. I was so happy, I cried. Anyway, I was riding around the neighborhood on my new Vespa, and I jumped it off a skateboard ramp that some neighborhood kids put out in the street.

I know it was crazy, but I just had to do it. Now my kids and all the boys on our street think I'm a stud.

What do you do for fun now?
I ride my Vespa! When the boys are in school, I ride my scooter all around town, to the library, to the YMCA, to meet friends for lunch, and to do errands. And I take it on the windy roads up in the hills where there aren't many cars. I feel so free gliding along the road with the wind against my face. I feel like an *Easy Rider* Mom riding along on her white pearlescent scooter without a care in the world.

Any plans for future fun?
My friends Jane, Shawn, and Natalie and I are having a slumber party. We're all very excited about it. We're going to bring our PJs and sleeping bags and make popcorn and stay up late talking and listening to music and who knows? Maybe tell scary stories. I can't wait! I haven't had a slumber party with girlfriends since I was a teenager.

What do you enjoy most about family life?
That I can be a kid with the kids. John and I have been taking the boys to a climbing gym. We've been learning how to climb and how to belay. We also take them on hikes where there's tree climbing and rock climbing. And we have skipping stone contests. And headstanding contests. (I'm the unbeaten champion.) We take them on bike rides and jump off curbs and skid in the dirt. It makes me feel young and also closer to them. But I enjoy being the grown-up, too. I love the quiet evening

hours, when we all curl up together and read. There's nothing in the world more beautiful than the quiet, dreamy looks on their faces as I read *Harry Potter* or *Charlie and the Chocolate Factory.* It stops time.

How do you see yourself at sixty? At seventy?

When I'm sixty . . . well, if I'm not too busy with grandkids, I'd like to always be learning new things. I'd like to go back to college and perfect my French. Maybe learn Italian. I'd like to learn how to brew beer and keep bees and maybe take up piano or guitar. There's so much I'd like to do and can't right now. So I'm looking forward to the later years when I'll have more time. I can see myself as some kind of globe-trotting grandma who spends the occasional summer writing poetry in French cafés or surfing in New Zealand and coming back with presents for the grandkids—providing I can afford all that!

When I'm seventy . . . well, I might slow down a little, but not too much. Gosh, I don't know! I hope I'm just like my mother. She's got more energy than most twenty-year-olds. Her house is always filled with friends and grandkids, and she's got a powerful love of life. She can laugh, and I couldn't ask for more than to laugh. Maybe, by seventy, I'll finally get to the long list of books I've always wanted to read. I'll install a comfortable chair in my garden and reread all of Shakespeare's plays. And I'll garden properly. I'll plant every square inch of my garden with flowers. I want hummingbirds, butterflies, and bees to be battling over every leaf. And I want to sit right in the middle of it and close my eyes and listen to all the wonderful noise.

About the Editor

Born and raised in Northern California, Indi Zeleny fled the nest and established brief homes from D.C. to London to Bangkok before settling back down in her birthplace along the coast, where she lives in the country with her husband Randy, two children, her mother, and assorted dogs and cats. For the last two decades, she spent much of her free time traveling, climbing, snowboarding, backpacking, scuba diving, and dancing—and recently embarked on the greatest epic of all: parenthood. Now, when she's not hanging with her family, working, or trying to eke out an hour or two of sleep, she tucks away into her office with its view of the rugged Santa Lucias, sipping Mexican hot chocolate and conjuring young-adult novels. Ardent adventurers, Indi and Randy have taken a hiatus from their beloved second- and third-world ramblings in order to ground school their two small hatchlings. Once they're fledged, the whole family will take to the skies.